*The
modern
presenter's
handbook*

The modern presenter's handbook

Jim R. Macnamara

PRENTICE HALL

Sydney   New York   Toronto   Mexico   New Delhi
London   Tokyo   Singapore   Rio de Janeiro

Acquisitions Editor: Kaylie Smith
Production Editor: Elizabeth Thomas
Cover design: Jack Jagtenberg
Typeset by Southern Star Design, South Tacoma, NSW
Printed in Australia by Australian Print Group, Victoria

1 2 3 4 5 00 99 98 97 96

ISBN 0 7248 0840 X

National Library of Australia
Cataloguing-in-Publication Data

Macnamara, Jim R.
   The modern presenter's handbook

   Bibliography
   Includes index
   ISBN 0 7248 0840 X

   1. Business presentations. 2. Public speaking. I. Title.

658.452

Prentice Hall of Australia Pty Ltd, *Sydney*
Prentice Hall, Inc., *Englewood Cliffs, New Jersey*
Prentice Hall Canada, Inc., *Toronto*
Prentice Hall Hispanoamericana, *SA, Mexico*
Prentice Hall of India Private Ltd, *New Delhi*
Prentice Hall International, Inc., *London*
Prentice Hall of Japan, Inc., *Tokyo*
Simon & Schuster (Asia) Pte Ltd, *Singapore*
Editora Prentice Hall do Brasil Ltda, *Rio de Janeiro*

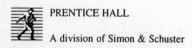

PRENTICE HALL

A division of Simon & Schuster

*t*able of contents

*a*bout the author

JIM MACNAMARA learned presentation skills firstly as a journalist working in radio, television and documentary film making. This provided a solid grounding in the techniques of speaking, appearing in front of audiences and using microphones, visual media and advanced presentation aids such as teleprompters.

After eight years as a journalist, he then pursued a successful career as a public relations executive and consultant where he gained extensive experience in speech writing, in organising public forums such as seminars and conferences, and in giving presentations.

Jim has given many hundreds of presentations as a spokesperson for companies and industry groups, as a public relations executive and as Chairman and CEO of his own company.

He has worked as a consultant and trainer with many leading national and international companies and organisations including Microsoft, Lotus Development, Compaq Computer, Dell Computer, Sony, Coca-Cola, UPS, BOC, Inchcape, Vodafone and Singapore Airlines.

His extensive work with some of the world's leading computer and communications companies has given him experience in the latest presentation technologies using personal computers, presentation software, data projectors, multimedia and interactive on-line services.

The author holds a Diploma in Journalism, a Bachelor of Arts (BA) in media studies and literary studies, and a Master of Arts (MA) by research in media and public relations.

Other books he has written include:

Public Relations Handbook for Clubs & Associations
Public Relations Handbook for Managers & Executives
The Australian Marketing & Promotion Handbook
How To Give Winning Presentations
The Asia Pacific Public Relations Handbook.

He is also co-author of the *New Zealand Handbook of Public Relations*.

*t*he *WorkWise series*

The *WorkWise* series will provide readers with the skills and techniques to improve personal and business productivity. Based on sound management principles, all the books in the series are written in a practical and easy-to-read style.

To enhance their easy-to-use format, the books are filled with practical ideas and illustrative examples which reinforce concepts and provide a handy and reliable resource for anyone interested in boosting their personal and business success.

The books in the *WorkWise* series will help anyone who is in the workforce, or looking to join the workforce, who is keen to improve their work skills with a view to enhancing their productivity and accomplishments.

Forthcoming titles in the series include:

time management
resume writing
telephone techniques
conducting meetings
self-motivation
supervision
performance appraisal
negotiation
writing a marketing plan
personal investment
working from home.

The *WorkWise* series is a joint publishing venture between the Australian Institute of Management (AIM) Training Centre and Prentice Hall Australia Pty Limited. Enquires about books in the series, or information regarding the submission of manuscripts, should be directed to either AIM or Prentice Hall.

*i*ntroduction

The Modern Presenter's Handbook is a practical guide packed with tips and 'how to' information for people who have to give speeches, reports, talks or lectures as part of their job—and especially for business executives and professionals who want, or are expected, to use modern presentation aids such as overheads, slides, electronic whiteboards, PC data projection, video conferencing and multimedia tools.

There are already many books about public speaking, but most focus predominantly, or only, on *speaking*. Today, business executives, professionals, trainers and teachers are increasingly required to present information that involves visual materials such as overhead transparencies and slides, computer data, video and, increasingly, multimedia.

Speaking utilises only one of our receptive senses—hearing. Human science tells us that only 11% of our information is received through hearing; 75% is received visually (Malouf, 1988, p. 81).

Presentations, as distinct from public speaking, use visual as well as audio communication. They also frequently utilise techniques such as demonstrations, interactive audience participation, humour, entertainment, drama and a range of other special techniques explained in this handbook.

This does not mean that giving presentations is overly difficult, or the domain of professionals only. Even showing a simple slide of a chart or graph, or telling a story, can help turn a boring speech into a presentation that will achieve your objectives.

Modern presentation aids help presenters as well as audiences by providing support for their message and prompts which they can refer to, as well as saving time in both preparation and delivery.

While assisting speakers in using modern presentation aids, this handbook also recaps the basics of good communication and public speaking techniques. No amount of technology will help if a presentation is poorly structured, not relevant to the audience, too long or lacking in some other respect. Presentation aids are not a substitute for good content and technique; they are additional tools to enhance and improve communication in presentations.

The *medium* should never become the *message*. But, used well, modern presentation aids can add impact, hold audience attention, increase retention and make you look more professional.

The tips and techniques outlined in this book are relevant to a wide range of presentation situations—staff meetings, report and proposal presentations at work, training courses and workshops, seminar and conference addresses, sales presentations, product launches, or professional presentations on the speaker circuit.

This is not a book to read once and put away. It contains numerous checklists for various steps and stages of planning, preparing and delivering presentations, as well as diagrams and even maps such as common audience seating arrangements. This book is designed as a practical reference to keep handy and to use whenever you want to give a successful presentation.

As far as practicable, this handbook is up to date with modern presentation aids and technology. Simple, practical explanations are given to guide presenters through the technical mysteries of equipment and facilities such as reverse projection, computer generated slides, PC data projection, teleprompters, infrared remote slide changers, and more.

Thus, this book is an invaluable companion for the modern presenter.

JIM R. MACNAMARA

The secret of successful presentations

A United States study of 10,000 people in various fields showed that, despite growth of the management sector and increasing education, 32% of respondents rated giving a speech in public as their greatest fear (*The Book of Lists* in Walters, 1989, p. 108). Fear of speaking in public rated ahead of financial problems, fear of heights and fear of death. In other words, one-third of people in the study said they would rather die than speak in public!

Many executives, supervisors, consultants, trainers and teachers face fear of embarrassment and failure in front of their peers, colleagues, customers, staff and other important groups because of lack of presentation skills.

Leading executive search firms and human resource specialists say that presentation skills are a key factor in career advancement, and advise that a lack of presentation skills may negatively affect promotion and new job opportunities.

A survey of male and female executives earning more than $250,000 a year by one of the top 10 executive search firms in the US, asked these high achievers to rank the factors which most contributed to their success. Both men and women ranked communication skills as the number one attribute which helped them achieve their position. Men ranked communication skills at 71%

(compared to 29% for formal education) while women put the figure at 89% (Matthews, 1994, p. 7).

In another business survey conducted by *USA Today*, 85% of business women rated communication skills as one of the most critical factors in their success (Morphew, 1994, p. 45).

A study by the APM Training Institute, a leading private business training organisation in Sydney, found the top three skills desired in marketing executives are communication-related. And guess what was number one? Presentation skills, rating a whopping 80.7% (Morphew, 1994, p. 46).

Carole Cowan, an Australian presentation skills trainer, says management's fears and the inability to communicate and present effectively also cost business millions of dollars a year. If you cannot win your shareholders' confidence at an annual general meeting, if you cannot get your proposal or plan accepted, if you cannot gain support when you deliver a report, or if you cannot stimulate loyalty from your staff when you talk to them, then your business will suffer.

Professor Di Yerbury, Vice Chancellor of Macquarie University in Sydney and a recognised industrial relations and communication specialist, says: 'Today, I would go so far as to say that we can't be good managers unless we're good at communicating with people' (Macnamara & Venton, 1990, p. 15).

If you don't consider yourself a good presenter or you feel there is room for improvement, there is good news from the outset. You can learn to be an effective presenter. Yes, anyone can. Giving presentations is a skill developed with training and practice. It does not come naturally even though some speakers make it look like a natural gift.

Niki Flacks, a former actress and creator of the Power Talk speaker training program, says: 'Public speaking is performing. It is not a natural activity that we should be good at from birth. Like acting, it is heightened communication and requires specific training' (Flacks & Rasberry, 1982, p. 5).

But a word of warning: 'performing' as a presenter does not mean that presentations are about being slick, glitzy or putting on a show. How you dress, smooth technique and attractive visuals are important elements of presentations. But looking good is not our ultimate goal. You can make a marvellous delivery and not achieve anything. Successful presentations are those that achieve objectives.

When you give a presentation, you want to initiate or influence a course of action. You may be presenting a report, a plan, a proposal, a sale, your candidature for office, or an idea. Whatever the subject of your presentation, you want to *win* something. At the very least, you want to win respect for your point of view.

In business, in organisations and in public life, our ability to generate action very often depends on our ability to present our ideas persuasively and convincingly.

Marketing your message

Even if you have overcome the fear of giving presentations, you can continue to learn new skills to better achieve your objectives and improve the communication effectiveness of your presentations.

You should not focus only on your own needs, such as overcoming nervousness. Your partner in the communication process during a presentation is the audience. What about them?

Christine Maher who founded the professional speakers' bureau, Celebrity Speakers, says there should be an RSPCA for people—A Royal Society for the Prevention of Cruelty to Audiences. Judging by the number of boring and tedious speeches that are given to conferences, seminars, annual general meetings, speech nights and business meetings each year, she is right.

Many speakers assume that their audience will listen to them. Some speakers even feel that the audience *has* to listen. After all, they are there in the room. They came along, didn't they? They may even have paid to attend. Senior executives often mistakenly feel that their staff will listen to them simply because they are the boss.

You can invite people into the room for a presentation. You can even compel them to attend in some cases. But you cannot force people to listen. And you certainly cannot force people to take in and retain or act on what you say. Common courtesy may prevent people actually walking out during your presentation. But that does not mean they are listening. They may 'walk out in their mind'.

In today's information satiated age, most of us have become expert at 'tuning out'. When a speaker is droning on, the audience may be thousands of kilometres away—lying on the beach in Bali, skiing in New Zealand, fantasising about the beautiful blonde or the handsome guy across the way, or back at the office solving some problem.

Some presentation trainers refer to this capacity for our minds to wander on to other things as 'Route 350' (see Figure 1.1). This term takes its name from communication psychology research findings which show that most people can listen and take in information at around 500 words per minute. But the average person can speak clearly only at around 150 words per minute. The difference—a mental capacity to process 350 words per minute—is channelled into other thoughts unless it is occupied by the speaker using some technique other than just speaking (Stuart, 1988, p. 2).

Christina Stuart, Managing Director of Speakeasy Training Ltd in the UK, which has trained thousands of professional men and women in giving presentations, says speakers have to win and hold their audience's attention—and regularly 'gather up the stragglers' who wander off down Route 350.

When you give a presentation, you have to *sell* your message. The audience is not a captive crowd just sitting there waiting for your pearls of wisdom. Most presenters seriously over-estimate the attentiveness of their audience.

'ROUTE 350'	
Human brain processes information	500 words per minute
Average speaking speed	150 words per minute
Unused mental capacity	350 words per minute

FIGURE 1.1 *Unused mental capacity is termed 'Route 350'*

An audience usually includes many people who would rather be somewhere else. Start with this assumption and you are on safe ground. You will approach the preparation and delivery of your presentation differently.

Some executives initially have trouble accepting this marketing or selling approach to giving presentations. However, as Robert Louis Stevenson said: 'Everyone lives by selling something' (Stuart, 1988, p. 190).

Mark McCormack, a highly successful businessman whose company, IMG, today manages many of the leading international sporting events including Wimbledon, quotes Boston Celtics coach, Red Auerbach, who used to say: 'It's not what you tell them that's important. It's what they hear' (McCormack, 1989, p. 191).

From the very outset, you need to put aside the view that a presentation is what you are going to say. It is what your audience is going to hear—and buy.

Successful presentations involve communication. Communication is a two-part process. The word communication comes from the Greek noun *communis* meaning a community or commonness, and the Latin verb *communicare* which means to build or create.

Communication is about 'creating a community' or commonness of understanding within a group. In other words, your message has to be delivered and received before communication has taken place. Far too much emphasis is placed by most presenters on what they are going to deliver and not enough on what the audience is going to receive.

The key to communication and marketing to any audience is that you have to show what's in it for them. There is a saying that everyone in the world listens to one radio station—WII-FM. What's in it for me?

Just as sales staff are taught to explain benefits and not product features, presenters need to tell their audiences the benefits that they will receive from a presentation. You have to market your presentation to make it appealing to the audience and then deliver on that promise.

4

The five Ps

If you accept that there is more to giving a successful presentation than arranging what you want to say and standing up and saying it, you will quickly see why so much emphasis is placed on preparation. Preparation is the underlying secret of all successful presentations. There is no way around it. There are no shortcuts. In presentations, preparation is everything.

A successful presentation is like an iceberg. The majestic sheet of ice or towering peak that we see and marvel at above the water is only the tip of the iceberg. Up to 90% of an iceberg lies below the surface. Without that base, the sheet of ice or peak would sink or topple over.

Ninety per cent of every successful presentation is below the surface in preparation.

In the army, recruits are taught 'the five Ps' as part of the basics for every drill they do:

O Proper
O Preparation
O Prevents
O Poor
O Performance.

You may be able to speak with authority on your subject, but you will need careful preparation for two key reasons:

1. If you know your subject well, or have researched it thoroughly, you will have far more information than the audience can digest in one presentation. You will need to sift the information and select the most salient points. (If you don't have a lot of information, you should not be presenting.)

2. Even if your subject material rolls off your tongue, you will need to plan how to 'market' it to your audience—how to gain and retain audience attention, how to establish audience relevance and answer WII-FM.

Presenting without proper planning is like shooting without aiming at a target. Bullets may be fired, but they will not hit anything. The net result is the same—a lot of noise but nothing for dinner!

Many presenters claim that they don't have time to prepare. Proper preparation does not necessarily mean that a presentation will take longer to produce. In fact, a well-prepared presentation is often quicker to put together in the end than one which emerges from a last-minute panic.

Abraham Lincoln said of preparation: 'If I had eight hours to chop down a tree, I'd spend six sharpening my ax' (Walters, 1989, p. 73).

Dale Carnegie, one of the most famous trainers of our time, said: 'A prepared speech is nine-tenths delivered' (Carnegie, 1957, p. 29).

There are major benefits for you as well as the audience from careful preparation:

○ first, preparation can save you time;

○ secondly, preparation is the first step to reducing nervousness and that feeling of 'butterflies' that occurs just before a presentation.

Most nervousness is not caused by the audience in front of you. It is caused by an inner fear that you will stand up and not know what to say. Speaker's lockjaw!

There is an old saying: 'The human brain is a wonderful thing. It starts the moment you are born and never stops until you stand up to speak in public.' Many presenters certainly feel this way. But preparation will dramatically change the way you approach presentations.

Of course, you need to do preparation in the right areas. This book outlines the eight steps to successful presentations and these steps are discussed in the next eight chapters, with a final chapter dealing with after a presentation. These eight steps follow the logical sequence of preparing and delivering a presentation, and explain in detail the preparation you should do to make every presentation a winner.

Eight steps to successful presentations

Figure 1.2 overviews the eight steps to successful presentations. These eight steps will be discussed in detail in the following chapters.

As shown in Figure 1.2, delivery of your presentation is the peak of the pyramid—the ultimate point that we will arrive at after the seven preceding steps.

You will observe that writing your script or speech is well along the way— step five in fact. There are many things to do before you start working out the words you want to say. You must resist the urge to jump right in and start writing a speech when you receive an invitation or request to make a presentation. However tempting, skipping over the essential steps of preparation will ultimately take longer and your presentation may fail.

Many would-be presenters believe subject knowledge is the main requirement for giving successful presentations, and indeed subject knowledge *is* a prerequisite for giving successful presentations. As shown in Figure 1.2, the pyramid diagram of the eight steps for successful presentations, subject knowledge underpins the whole structure. It is the foundation of presentations.

But subject knowledge is not enough on its own. Being an expert in a particular subject does not necessarily mean someone can give interesting, effective presentations about that subject. Certainly you should have sufficient knowledge about your subject to give a presentation. But we will return later to see how beginning at step one and following the eight steps to successful

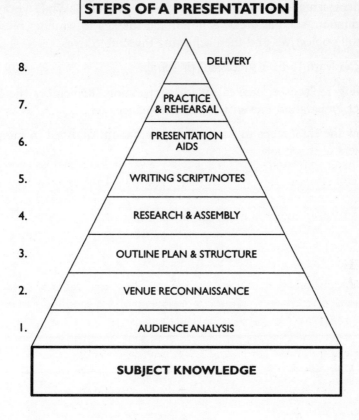

STEPS OF A PRESENTATION

8. DELIVERY

7. PRACTICE & REHEARSAL

6. PRESENTATION AIDS

5. WRITING SCRIPT/NOTES

4. RESEARCH & ASSEMBLY

3. OUTLINE PLAN & STRUCTURE

2. VENUE RECONNAISSANCE

1. AUDIENCE ANALYSIS

SUBJECT KNOWLEDGE

FIGURE 1.2 *Eight steps to successful presentations*

presentations will result in selecting the right pieces of subject knowledge for the audience and how to use this knowledge in the optimum way.

Summary

○ Most presenters over-estimate the attentiveness of their audience. Usually an audience is made up of people who would rather be somewhere else. You have to sell yourself and your message in every presentation.

○ Far too much emphasis is placed by most presenters on what they are going to deliver—and not enough on what the audience is going to receive. Delivery is only half of a presentation. Communication is a two-part process, involving delivery of a message and reception of that message. You have to ensure your audience receives your message, otherwise no communication has taken place and you are wasting your time.

○ Good presentations are not about gloss and glitter. While your physical presentation, such as dress, is important, the key to winning presentations is setting objectives and then achieving those objectives.

○ You can learn to be a successful presenter.

○ Nothing replaces or makes up for preparation. Remember the five Ps—Proper Preparation Prevents Poor Performance.

○ Follow the eight steps to successful presentations outlined in the following chapters of this book.

2

Audience analysis

In marketing we are taught that the customer is king or queen. Marketers spend millions of dollars on market research to understand consumers—their audience. They recognise that, unless they know everything possible about the people to whom they are trying to sell, their marketing messages are likely to miss their mark and their campaigns will fail.

As discussed in Chapter 1, when we give a presentation, we are trying to sell something to an audience. We may be selling a plan or proposal, our ideas, a training message to improve productivity, a motivational message, or 'pitching' for new business. In both marketing and communication, one rule is fundamental: *know thine audience*.

Too many presenters charge into preparing their presentation thinking about all the things they would like to say. Put your subject material aside for the moment. Presentations start where we want them to end up—with the audience.

You need to know all you possibly can about your audience before you put even one word on paper. Long before you think about a title for your presentation, before you start making slides, even before you start jotting down ideas on a pad or sketching an outline, you need to get inside the heads of your audience.

Who, what, where, when, why and how?

Journalists are taught to ask six key questions when writing a story. This formula was expressed in a verse by Rudyard Kipling entitled 'The Journalist's Six Friends' (Walters, 1989, p. 56):

> *'I keep six honest serving men,*
> *They taught me all I knew*
> *Their names are What and Where and When*
> *And How and Why and Who.'*

It does not matter in what order you consider these important questions, but you should work through the following audience analysis checklist before every presentation:

O WHO is the audience? Understanding to whom you are presenting is termed audience analysis. You should know as much about your audience as possible—and not just generalities. Get specifics. Ask questions. Request background information be sent to you.
   —Is your audience comprised of union workers, farmers, sales executives, financial advisers, CEOs or a 'mixed bag'?
   —Are they mostly men, women or both?
   —Are they old, young, middle-aged?
   —What do they know about your subject?
   —How many people will be in the audience?

   Your message should be structured to suit the audience. Also, your language, tone, examples and even any jokes you tell should be keyed carefully to your audience. You can only do this if you know who they are.

O WHAT does the audience want to know about? What do they want to hear? What are their interests—as opposed to what you want to talk about? Ensure that what you plan to talk about is the same thing as the organisers and the audience want and expect.
   —Check the program. Often what is advertised may be different from what you are planning.
   —Make sure you receive a proper brief from the organisers on your presentation. This should include briefing you on other presenters and their topics. You don't want to repeat what another has said.

O WHERE are you delivering the presentation?
   —Which city or town?
   —Which venue?
   —Is the venue air-conditioned? In summer, this will be important for your audience.

—Will you be speaking after dinner or lunch?

—Will you be speaking from a lectern, from a table, from a stage, etc?

○ WHEN is the presentation?

—What day?

—What date?

—And, importantly, at what time?

What does the time of day have to do with audience analysis? Well, your audience will be in a different state of attentiveness at various times of day. For instance, if you are scheduled to present late in the afternoon (termed the 'graveyard shift'), your audience will have passed its attentiveness peak and will be anxious to go for a drink or go home. Some may leave early. Others may leave mentally—down Route 350!

AUDIENCE ANALYSIS

Who? ....

What? ....

Where? ....

When? ....

Why? ....

How? ....

Another challenging time to present is immediately after lunch, particularly if heavy food or alcohol has been served. It is becoming increasingly common to serve only light lunches with no alcohol at conferences, seminars and training workshops as it is recognised that audiences are likely to 'doze off' when seated in a closed room after a meal and a few glasses of alcohol.

If the time does not suit you, talk to the organisers. If there is no resolution and it looks like you are wasting your time, don't give the presentation.

O   WHY are you giving the presentation.
—Are you the right person?
—Do you have enough information about the subject?
—Is the subject something you feel strongly about or want to present on?
—Are you passionate about it?

Know why you are presenting.

O   HOW will you present?
—How long should the presentation be?
—Will you speak from notes, a full script, use overhead transparencies, slides, etc?
—Do you need special seating or venue arrangements such as an aisle down the middle to walk through or to position a projector?

In all of these questions it is important to get specifics. The more information you have, the more prepared you will be.

Many presentations that fail do so because they do not relate sufficiently to the audience. This occurs when this first step—audience analysis—has not been carried out carefully and thoroughly.

When you hear a presenter tell a joke that goes down badly or offends an audience, it is generally because he or she did not do proper audience analysis.

When a subject fails to excite or interest an audience it is usually not because of the subject or even the presenter's subject knowledge. It is usually because the subject material was not made relevant. Audiences will forgive you for nervous stumbles. They will even forgive you for losing your place. But they will not forgive you for failing to understand them and their needs.

Subject knowledge was discussed in Chapter 1 and positioned as the foundation of the presentation pyramid model, not as one of the steps. You should begin to see now why a presenter should not start with his or her subject knowledge. If you start with your own knowledge, you are preparing what *you* want to say. You will not know what information to select for your audience. By doing audience analysis and getting to understand the audience as the first step, you are then in a position to select information from your subject knowledge that will be relevant—not just to you, but to your audience.

So audience analysis is the first vital step in preparing for a presentation. And you should do it as thoroughly as possible. Every minute spent doing audience analysis will reward you twice over in time saved and impact gained later when you are up on the stage or podium presenting.

You can do audience analysis by:

O talking to the organisers and asking them questions—either in person or by phone;

O asking for a list of attendees. You may know some of them and this will help you relate and 'psych into' your audience;

O reading background information about the organisation or company if you are presenting to a particular group;

O reading press clippings about issues or the industry in which your audience is involved;

O calling up friends or contacts in the same industry or sector as your audience and asking them to background you.

By doing this early preparation, you will be in a much better position to prepare a successful presentation.

Many speakers, even professionals, carefully fill out an audience profile before every presentation. This can be done on a sheet of paper, or by using a form to prompt you to ask all the necessary questions about your audience.

Try using the audience profile form provided at the end of this chapter, or adapt it to your specific needs.

Summary

O The first step in preparing a presentation is to learn everything you can about your audience. Resist the temptation to skip over this step. Jokes flop, stories fall flat, examples don't work and key messages go over the heads of audiences when presenters don't do careful audience analysis. Discipline yourself to do this first step diligently every time and you will see a big difference in reaction to your presentations.

O Knowing generalities is not enough. You must know as many specifics as possible about your audience—their interests, education level, social background, political leanings—even whom they barrack for in football or basketball.

○ Doing audience analysis before choosing information from your subject knowledge and before planning your presentation will result in your message being tuned directly to the interests of your audience.

AUDIENCE PROFILE

Size: ....

Main groups: ....

....

....

....

Men/women balance: ....

Average age: ....

Education level (technical, blue-collar, academics, etc):

....

Occupations/specialist nature of group (eg, farmers, veterinarians, business people, etc):

....

....

Regional interests (eg, local town, city, State, etc):

....

....

....

continued...

Time of day of presentation (eg, will they be fresh and attentive, or tired?):

....

Seating (at tables so they can take notes, theatre style, etc):

....

The main things that people in this audience want to know/would be interested in:

1. ....

....

....

....

2. ....

....

....

....

3. ....

....

....

....

3

Venue reconnaissance

An alarming percentage of speakers walk into a room to deliver a presentation without ever having been to the venue previously. It is little wonder that they don't know where the switch is on the overhead projector, that they find the microphone on the lectern is pointing either at their forehead or at their navel and that their first words—or nervous, throat-clearing coughs—send an ear-piercing screech through the public address system.

Sound familiar? One of the best ways of becoming a good presenter is by being a recipient of presentations. You soon see what *not* to do. And one major 'must not do' is walking into a venue cold to give a presentation. From the outset, you will be feeling more nervous. And so you should be because unless you have checked out the venue and become comfortable with the room and equipment, there is a very high likelihood that things are going to go wrong.

After knowing your audience, knowing your venue is the next most important step to giving a successful presentation. When you stand up to present, you want to be able to focus your entire attention on your audience and on your presentation. You cannot do this if you are worrying about the microphone, how to dim the lights, or whether the overhead projector will work.

'Murphy's Law' is a principle which holds that if something can go wrong, it will go wrong. Murphy lives in presentation venues all over the world. Something is always bound to go wrong. The lights won't dim and will wash out your slides or overheads on the screen. Music will start playing through the hotel public address system in the middle of your presentation. The maintenance department will start drilling through masonry on the floor right above you just as you begin.

If you don't do venue reconnaissance, Murphy's Law will invariably apply. Even if you manage to fix them on the spot, last minute adjustments and negotiations about the venue leave you nervous, breathless and distracted—hardly the mindset to begin an important presentation. Those minutes immediately prior to a presentation should be used for a final glance over your notes and to sit calmly and 'psych' yourself up.

Whenever possible, you should carry out reconnaissance including a personal site inspection of the venue where you are to deliver a presentation. Clearly, this may not be practical if the venue is in another city or overseas. However, most major venues have printed floor plans and lists of equipment and facilities which they can mail or fax to you. If the venue is a hotel, talk to the Banquet Manager on the phone. If your venue is in an office, such as a boardroom, ask if you can check out the room several weeks or days in advance. As a last resort, if you cannot visit your venue in advance, ask if you can arrive early and gain access to the room an hour or more before your presentation.

This chapter discusses the major points to understand and to check in relation to the venue.

Seating and room layout

There are six main types of seating arrangements for meetings and conferences, generally described as:

O   theatre style (with or without aisles);

O   classroom style;

O   discussion style;

O   meeting style;

O   workshop style;

O   informal discussion style.

In some situations, you may not have a say in the seating and room layout. In other cases, you may be able to specify how the room is arranged. In any case, you need to understand how the room is set up before going too far in preparing a presentation.

For instance, if you are planning to use slides or overhead transparencies, you will need to ensure that there is space for the projector. If you plan to conduct an exercise that requires participants to write, they will need tables.

Each type of seating arrangement has advantages and disadvantages. If your audience is seated at round tables, some may have their backs to you and will need to swivel around to see you or a screen.

Figure 3.1 shows some of the most popular seating arrangements to assist you in planning your room layout.

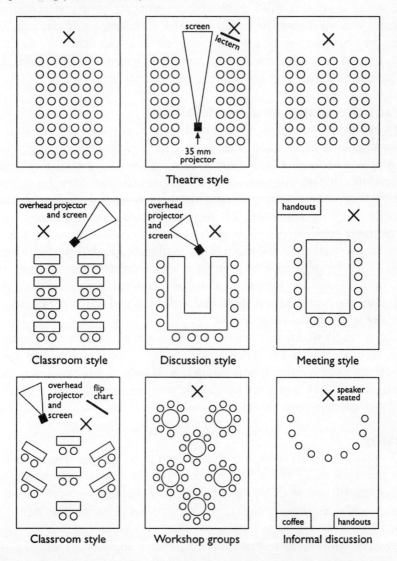

FIGURE 3.1 *Major types of seating arrangements* (Christina Stuart, 1988)

Most large audiences are arranged theatre style. One or more aisles may be provided to allow easy access. Theatre style arrangements generally suit a formal presentation. Smaller classroom, meeting room, workshop and informal discussion group layouts suit a more intimate approach.

The type that is not shown in these diagrams is the dinner speech format. However, it usually follows the workshop group layout and the tone is formal.

Always find out the proposed room layout and seating arrangements in advance, as part of venue reconnaissance. And don't be afraid to ask for changes. Often, venue organisers will be able to accommodate your preferences. At the very least, you will know the 'lay of the land' in advance and can plan around it. You won't have any surprises when you arrive at your venue.

Don't try to remember the various seating arrangements. If it helps, photocopy the one you want and fax it to the venue organiser.

Air-conditioning and ventilation

Along with seating arrangements, the next most important aspect of your venue is the temperature of the room. The most comfortable median temperature for most people is between 22–23 degrees Celsius (68–70 degrees Fahrenheit).

When the temperature rises above 24 degrees Celsius, drowsiness sets in— especially if combined with a droning speaker's voice and subdued lighting. If the temperature is less than 21 degrees Celsius, your audience will be uncomfortably cold.

However, a good tip if the room is air-conditioned is to turn the control to a slightly lower temperature than normal before a presentation or event begins. Warm bodies and hot lamps in slide or overhead projectors increase the temperature of a room. So you should allow for this and start a presentation with the room slightly colder than normal.

If the room in which you are presenting is not air-conditioned, ensure that there is adequate ventilation. You may have to leave doors or windows open, but check on any outside noise before doing this. If there is a busy freeway outside, or construction work going on next door, you may have to resort to fans and leave doors and windows closed.

Lighting

Another vitally important aspect of your venue is lighting. Hotel conference rooms and even many office boardrooms, training rooms and meeting rooms have not caught up with the technological revolution and fail to cater for overhead, slide or video projection which often requires the lights to be dimmed.

Very often venue lights will be controlled from a single switch which gives you either full white-out on your screen or pitch black. Many hotels seem to specialise in having bright spotlights that shine not only on the speaker, but directly on to the screen. You need to know this kind of information in advance before turning up with your carousel of expensive, painstakingly produced slides.

You should not turn off or dim lights to the extent that your audience is sitting in gloom or dark. A dark room will hasten the onset of drowsiness, it will diminish your ability to make eye contact with your audience and it will prevent attendees writing notes which can be extremely frustrating and counter-productive for your presentation.

Fortunately, being able to dim lighting is not the major issue it once was with the development of high wattage, high resolution projectors. These will be discussed in Chapter 7 which deals with presentation aids.

But it is still preferable to have some control over your lighting and you should check this out during venue reconnaissance. Modern, purpose-built presentation venues have sophisticated lighting controls which enable you to dim or turn off lights which shine on the screen and leave sufficient lighting above the audience for them to feel comfortable and write notes. You should also ensure that you are standing in the light so the audience can see you clearly.

If you don't have suitable lighting controls, there are shortcuts and 'tricks of the trade' which can help you achieve the right lighting for your presentation. For instance, removing a few bulbs in strategic locations will remove direct 'wash' on your screen and allow you to leave the lights on.

Also, don't forget nature's light. Check that there are drapes on the windows if you are presenting in a room exposed to sunlight. Bright sunlight can flood a room at certain times of the day and, unless there are drapes, it can make projection of slides, overheads or video nearly impossible.

Lecterns

Most presentations are made from a lectern, although many business presenters and trainers are moving away from lecterns as they can make you appear remote from your audience. Behind a lectern, a presenter can become like a preacher in a pulpit. And there is always the tendency to cling to the lectern like a drowning person clutching a life raft.

However, until you are fully comfortable 'working a room' by walking around or standing directly in front of your audience, you will most commonly use a lectern and you should become familiar with this aspect of your venue.

In most cases, the lectern will already be in place when you arrive at a venue and you will have little say in the type. However, you should carefully note and look for the following facilities:

O Is there a height adjustment? Know where it is and ensure the lectern is at the correct height for you.

○ Does it have a script light? If so, does it work? Know where the switch is located.

○ Does the microphone pick up every bump on the lectern and the rustling of your papers? Note microphone sensitivity and be careful not to feed unwanted sound into the PA system.

○ What controls are available on the lectern and where are they?

New generation lecterns are highly advanced. Many feature in-built control systems for operating lights, slides and even curtains or drapes. If you are using a new 'high tech' lectern, check out the controls during venue reconnaissance. Otherwise, you may face confusion and embarrassment during your presentation.

A major presentation at Compaq Computer, a very professional company, once went terribly wrong when the presenter using a new remote control system for the first time had the drapes around the room opening and closing every time he tried to change slides. Before long the presentation dissolved into uncontrollable laughter. It was a memorable presentation, but all most attendees remembered were the flying drapes, not the content of the presentation.

Screen position

If you are projecting images as part of your presentation, the screen should be sufficiently large and positioned so that the audience is at no greater angle than 45 degrees to the screen.

Ensure your audience is not too far away. Conversely, make sure they are not too close to the screen at the front. A guideline recommended by Kodak is that the first row of seats should be no closer than twice the width of the screen. So, for example, if you are using a two metre wide screen (approximately six feet), your first row of seats should be no closer than four metres (12-15 feet).

Make sure you use the right type of screen for the venue. Yes, there is more than one type of screen. (See equipment for presentations discussed in Chapter 7.)

Projector position

Siting of projectors is one of the most important decisions in delivering a presentation with visual support. Many presenters leave this until they arrive at the venue. This is asking for trouble, as projectors usually need to be located at precise locations depending on type and lens focal length.

An overhead projector almost always has to be sited directly in front of and close to the screen. However, you can have flexibility with slide and video projectors.

You can improve your presentation by positioning slide and video projectors out of sight of the audience—or at least out of their direct line of vision. For instance, using reverse projection will put all your projection equipment behind the screen and is highly recommended if possible in your venue. However, you will require sufficient projection distance behind the screen—usually three to four metres.

Slide projectors can be located in a projection room or 'bio-box' at the back of the room if the venue has such a facility. Alternatively, they can be located on a stand at the rear, in an aisle or a corner. If a slide projector has been set up at the back of the room, you will need to check that it is fitted with a telephoto lens of the correct length to project on to a screen at the front.

Likewise, if you are using an overhead projector and intend changing transparencies yourself, check if there is a stage and measure the distance from the lectern to the projector. Don't be like the speaker who turned up to give a presentation with overheads only to find himself standing on a one metre high stage with the overhead projector on the floor below him and the steps on the far side of the stage. That's when the butterflies really start to flap their wings.

Video projectors can be ceiling-mounted and many venues now have projectors installed this way.

Power supply

Know the location of power points if you are using equipment such as an overhead, slide or video projector. Murphy's Law means that the power point will often be on the other side of the room from where you need it, and your lead will be just a few centimetres or inches short.

Many presenters carry their own extension lead around with them along with other 'goodies' such as spare bulbs and double adaptors or power boards.

If you are travelling overseas for a presentation, check the type of power points used. Plugs vary from country to country. Special adaptors are available which will enable you to plug your equipment in to most systems used worldwide. If you cannot find them locally, airport duty free shops almost always sell adaptors.

Even more importantly, check the voltage used in any country you are visiting. The US uses 110 volt electricity, the UK and Australia use 240 volt, while many European and Asian countries use 220 or 230 volt. You may need special adaptors to handle different voltages.

Usually the range of acceptable voltage is printed on equipment labels. Most equipment used by presenters will handle a range of 110–240 volts. But it is best to be sure. The smell of smoke coming from your projector is not a happy start to your presentation.

Public address system

Public address or PA systems are another source of fear for presenters. We have all been to weddings and other social functions where the PA 'pops' and hisses and emits ear-piercing screeches. Nothing is more disruptive for a presenter and an audience than a sound system that acts up.

Usually, however, the fault is human error. You need to know how close to speak into the PA system for optimum effect. You can only achieve this through venue reconnaissance. It's too late for experimenting when you stand up to present.

Inexperienced speakers compound the problem of PA systems by tapping or blowing on the microphone to see if it is working. Don't. It is pre-set for voice. Tapping or blowing will treat your audience to sounds like gunshots or the snorts of a beast from *Jurassic Park*.

As with screens and lighting, audio amplification technology has marched forward and the types of PA systems used in most business and conference situations today are advanced, user-friendly and relatively idiot-proof. But always test the PA system as part of your venue reconnaissance. (See important information about microphones in Chapter 7.)

Outside distractions

It is also important to find out if there are likely to be any outside distractions at the time of your presentation. Check the following:

O   Is the building undergoing renovations?

O   Is there a construction site next door?

O   Is there a busy freeway outside?

O   Are there low-flying aircraft in the area?

O   Is the room next door to the kitchen? (Kitchens in major hotels and conference centres can be very noisy.)

O   Is there any equipment in use near the venue that will cause a disturbance such as power drills, jackhammers, etc?

I once arrived in a hall in a small town for a talk to a group of farmers. I had checked the room the evening before and gone to great lengths to prepare a stimulating presentation which was due at 9 o'clock the next morning.

However, just before I began my presentation, loud jackhammering erupted right outside the building, reverberating through the room and drowning out most of what the chairman was saying. I had not checked outside during my venue reconnaissance. Had I done so, I would have noticed renovations under way on the building. It really does pay to do thorough venue reconnaissance.

Refreshments

A final suggestion for venue reconnaissance is to check on refreshments that are available for your audience. Refreshments such as tea and coffee help an audience maintain attentiveness. Consider whether you want tea and coffee served only at breaks, or whether you want these refreshments on a table at the back of the room so audience members can help themselves at any time. This is a common approach in workshops and informal meetings.

In most countries it is a good tip to ensure that there is water on the table. A cold glass of water can be refreshing, particularly if the room becomes overly warm. And, while you are at it, make sure there is a glass of water available to you in case you get a dry throat during your presentation.

Chewing has a stimulating effect on the body and can help people remain attentive, so many venue organisers provide mints or some other form of confectionary for audiences. Remember, the first step of successful presentations is focusing on your audience, not just on yourself and what you want to say.

Thoroughly checking out every aspect of your venue is a vital part of preparing a successful presentation. Don't leave this key element of preparation to chance. Some presenters walk around with a clip-board and a checklist of venue requirements before every presentation.

Make the venue your turf. One leading speaker says that before he gets up to speak he 'owns' the room. 'It's mine,' he says. He has been over every aspect of the venue and feels confident that it will work for him and there are no surprises. That way, when you stand up to present, you can focus on your audience and your message.

To assist you, this handbook provides a number of checklists including a checklist for venue reconnaissance. Try it.

CHECKLIST FOR
VENUE RECONNAISSANCE

○ **Seating format**

　—What is the seating format?
　—Do you want theatre, classroom, meeting, discussion, workshop or informal discussion style?
　—Do you have any special requirements (eg, aisles to walk around or for audience access, a top table, a second lectern for a co-presenter)?

○ **Lighting**

　—Are the lights fitted with dimmers?
　—Are there any lights that shine directly on the screen?
　—Do these have separate switches so you can turn them off? Check the switches.

continued ...

—Organise to have someone operate the lights if possible.

—Are there curtains to block sunlight if it is a bright room? (Don't forget to consider sunlight and ask questions if you are making an evening inspection and the presentation is to be during the day.)

○ **Lectern**

—Is there a lectern?

—Is it a standard type or modern electronic type?

—Is the height adjustable? If so, check how it adjusts. (The speaker before you could be a giant or a midget.)

—Does it have a script light? Check that the bulb works.

—Does it have projector controls for slides?

—Check if the lectern is sensitive to the PA system. Are turning your papers or touching the lectern amplified through the PA?

○ **Microphone and PA system**

—What type of microphone is provided—on the lectern, separate stand, hand-held or neck microphone (see 'Microphones' in Chapter 7)?

—Is it permanently turned on, or do you have to turn it on?

—Is it the correct volume? Test it.

—Does it 'pop' or 'hiss' when you speak closely to it? If it does, ask for it to be adjusted.

—Does it screech if you speak closely? If it does, stand back, or ask for it to be adjusted.

○ **Screen**

—Is there an in-built screen (eg, wall-mounted or ceiling-lowered), or do you need to bring in a portable screen?

—Check the operation of the in-built screen. Ensure there are no cuts or tears and that the lowering mechanism works if applicable.

—Is it a suitable type of screen for your needs?

—Is it large enough for the audience?

○ **Screen position**

—Is the screen at no more than a 45 degree angle to any part of the audience so they can see it properly?

—Is it properly located in relation to the projector/s?

○ **Projectors**

—Is there a projection box built in at the back of the room? (This is sometimes called a bio-box.)

—Alternatively, will you reverse project? Ensure there is adequate projection length behind the screen if you plan to do this.

continued...

—Where will you site your projector if it is free standing? Is there a suitable aisle or area where it will not block the audience's view and distract people?

o **Control switches**

—Do you know the location of all control switches for sound volume, lights, lectern height etc?

o **Power supply**

—Do you know where power points are located?
—Are they close enough to your equipment?
—Do you need an extension lead or power board?
—For overseas presenters, check whether it is 110, 220 or 240 volt power and ensure your equipment is compatible.

o **Other equipment**

—Do you require any other equipment, such as a flip chart, whiteboard, overhead projector, pointer, extra carousels for slides, spare bulbs, table or stand for the projector, etc?

o **General**

—Is there any outside noise that will disturb or distract your audience (eg, a construction site adjacent or renovation work going on next door)? Ask about any work scheduled for the time of your presentation.
—Are there any pillars in the room which will block the audience's view?
—Are all cables taped down so they cannot be kicked out or dislodged, disconnecting your equipment? Masking tape will do a fine job of securing cables.
—Is there a technician in the venue? If so, introduce yourself and ask for his or her help. Technical people are usually only too happy to assist if asked.
—If you want a glass of water at the lectern, don't forget to ask.

Summary

o Always carry out a reconnaissance of your venue before your presentation. Inspect it personally whenever possible.

o If the venue is interstate or overseas, ask for floor plans and lists of specifications of equipment and facilities to be mailed or faxed to you.

o Use the checklist for venue reconnaissance provided to check out every aspect of the venue. Especially check:
—the seating arrangement and room layout—do they suit your needs? Ask for any additional things you need, such as a top table, or an aisle;

—what type of equipment you will be using;
—lighting (how much? is there sunlight?);
—where your projector can be located;
—whether there is a suitable screen and where it is located;
—will everyone in the audience be able to see your visuals?

4

Outline plan and structure

Once you have completed audience analysis and venue reconnaissance, you have a fairly good idea of what your audience is interested in, what they want to hear, the time and day of the presentation and the physical characteristics of the venue.

You will know any limitations such as lighting which may prevent the use of slides, the height of the stage which may mean you need an assistant to change overheads, the length of your presentation and whether the venue has the equipment you need.

Now you can start reviewing your subject knowledge and selecting the information that is best suited. Of course you will present what *you* consider the audience should be told. But, by having the audience and venue in mind, you will also select information that is relevant. And you will be much more likely to present it in a way which is carefully tuned to the particular audience and venue.

Every minute spent before this in audience analysis and venue reconnaissance has been well spent and will save you time in this stage of preparing your presentation. If you skipped over the first three chapters, you should go back at this point as everything discussed from here on will be based on what was covered earlier.

Setting your objectives

The first step of preparing an outline plan and structure for your presentation is to set objectives. You may have one or several objectives. For example, typical objectives of presentations are:

O   to show shareholders that the company is well managed and a profitable place for their continued investment;

O   to motivate staff to achieve higher levels of productivity;

O   to foster team-building, to increase morale and to enhance corporate culture;

O   to create wide awareness of, and support for, a policy;

O   to 'sell' a proposal or plan;

O   to successfully launch a new product.

Setting objectives is important because, unless we consciously identify what we want to achieve in a presentation, our objective subconsciously becomes 'to survive'. Some presenters openly admit that they just want to get through it. That is hardly a productive or ideal objective.

The objectives of your presentation should be relevant for the audience. And they should be realistic. You are unlikely, for instance, to be able to explain the complete operations of a company or organisation in one 30 minute presentation. Rather, you may have to focus on the main aspects which are relevant to the audience and simply summarise others.

Once you have clear objectives, you can then start to rough out a skeleton or structure of your presentation. What is it going to cover? What are the main parts? What will be the key messages or points?

Structure of presentations

There is no one rule for how a presentation should be structured. However, there is almost universal agreement that a presentation must have a structure. If you simply collect a large amount of information and attempt to work through it, you will wander off the subject, leave some parts out altogether, and probably confuse your audience.

There are many recommended structures for presentations. Some list as many as five components or sections. One of the most simple, but quite effective, structures to follow is a three-part format which presents a variation on the novelist's description of writing a book based around 'a beginning, a middle and an end'. This prescribes that a presentation should be comprised of:

O   an opening;

O   a main body; and

O   a conclusion.

A simple formula that will help you remember this basic structure and serve you well for many types of presentations allegedly owes its origins to Winston Churchill. It describes the three functions or parts of a presentation as:

1.   Tell 'em what you're gonna tell 'em.

2.   Tell 'em.

3.   Tell 'em what you've told 'em.

While you might think this sounds a little trite or low-brow as a formula for giving a presentation to your annual general meeting of shareholders, or outlining a major new proposal, this structure contains vital elements of effective communication.

Doug Malouf, in *How to Create and Deliver a Dynamic Presentation*, proposes the ERS Formula—Explain, Reinforce and Sell (Malouf, 1988, p. 36). This presents a variation on the 'Tell 'em' format and could be summarised as: 'Tell 'em; Tell 'em what you've told 'em; and Sell 'em'. It is noteworthy that Malouf's formula emphatically mentions *selling* which was discussed in Chapter 1. It reminds us that in presentations we are selling something. We have to market our message.

We will work through each of these key parts of a presentation in this chapter.

The opening

The opening of a presentation should do three things.

1.   *Grab attention*
    First, you have to grab the audience's attention. Research shows that most people form an opinion about someone in the first 30 seconds of contact. If you have a waffling five minute intro, you are dead in the water before you begin. The first few minutes are critical.
    Ed Wohlmuth, author of one of the best-selling speakers' books of all time, *The Overnight Guide to Public Speaking*, said a presenter had to send six signals to his or her audience (Wohlmuth, 1983, p. 38). Four of these must occur in the opening and one in each of the main body and the conclusion. Ed Wohlmuth's six signals that you should send to your audience are:

    —I will not waste your time;
    —I know who you are;
    —I am well organised;
    —I know my subject;

—Here is my most important point;

—I am finished.

George Jessel said: 'If you haven't struck oil in the first two or three minutes, stop boring' (Stuart, 1988, p. 98).

2. ***Tell them where you are going***

Secondly, your opening should tell the audience what you are going to talk about. This is necessary to orientate people. No one likes sitting in a room not knowing what is going to happen. People like to have 'sign posts' that say this is where we are heading.

By overviewing what you are going to talk about, you whet your audience's appetite and draw them into the subject. Provided you choose your words well, you create anticipation.

3. ***Sell them***

Thirdly, your opening should sell the audience on why they should listen. It should tell them what's in it for them to establish relevance. Remember WII-FM?

One leading trainer opens his sessions for sales executives with introductions such as: 'Today I am going to show you how to increase your commissions by 30%.'

It is simple. It is short. But he has their attention. The opening goes right to their 'hot buttons' and tells them what's in it for them.

There are many ways to open a presentation. Here are just some suggestions taken from the experience of many presenters:

○ Tell 'em what you're gonna tell 'em—simply state the purpose of your presentation (eg, 'Today I am going to show you how you can increase productivity and improve your customer service with the new System 5000').

○ Make a strong, controversial statement—then clarify it. This will always get audience attention.

○ Define a problem—for which the balance of your presentation will prescribe the solution.

○ Ask a real question requiring a show of hands or an answer from the audience.

○ Ask a rhetorical question (although this is dated and over-used).

○ Use a quotation (but not a common one or cliche).

○ Tell a story relevant to the audience to create empathy (this is good, provided you can tell stories in an interesting way).

○ Tell a joke (risky, but warms up the audience).

○ Get the audience to do something such as stand up and perform some exercise (difficult to control, but an effective stimulant).

○ Show a video (not generally recommended first up as you should establish yourself first).

○ Do something unusual such as a magic trick, staging effects, a demonstration, or use actors.

Once you have gained your audience's attention, signalled to them what you are going to talk about and described how it is relevant to them, you should move straight into the main body of your presentation.

The main body

The main body should present the points you want to make in a logical, well-connected way. As the name suggests, this is the main part of your presentation.

However, it is important that the main body is not presented as one large lump of information, facts and commentary. There are two important reasons why you should structure your main body in a number of sub-sections.

First, it is nearly impossible for any presenter to remember one long 20 or 30 minute dialogue. Breaking it into discrete parts enables you to deal with one at a time. At any one time, you need only remember three or four minutes of your presentation. When you finish that part, you can glance at your notes to remind yourself of the next point you want to discuss. Thus, breaking your main body down into sections makes your job as a presenter easier.

The second reason also has to do with memory—the audience's. Human memory works by storing 'chunks' of information in much the same way as a computer writes data to a disk. When you command a computer to save, copy or transfer a large file, it does not try to 'read' the entire file into memory (called Random Access Memory or RAM in a computer) and then write or send that file. A computer takes chunks of information or data and writes or sends that data one chunk at a time. Our memory works in much the same way. We take a chunk of information and store it in a relevant compartment of our brain, then go back for another chunk.

So you will not only make your task as a presenter easier, but you will increase audience understanding and retention by breaking the main body of your presentation down into digestible chunks of information. A main body of 20 to 30 minutes should be comprised of three to five chunks or sections. These chunks could be the three, four or five main points you want to make about the topic, the divisions or groups in your organisation, or some other logical breakdown.

Even presenters who know their subject well sometimes have trouble in assembling the main body of a script because they cannot decide the order in which to deal with material. It will help to know the main structures commonly identified and taught for arranging presentation material:

○ *Chronological*
As the term suggests, points can be arranged in order of occurrence. This is an ideal structure for describing a process, such as a production chain or flow chart of a distribution system. While easy to use, this structure has the disadvantage that it does not necessarily cover your points in order of importance.

○ *Spatial*
This presents points and ideas as they relate to each other. You can begin with the general and move to the particular. Or you can work from the big picture down to how it affects the individual or members of the audience. Another variation on this structure is the theory/practice model which presents the theory and then moves to discuss its implementation.

○ *Logical*
Several different patterns are used in a logical sequence. Points may be discussed by region or area, for instance. A logical sequence also could be to present problems followed by their solutions, or cause and effect.

○ *Topical*
Also known as the qualitative structure, this approach deals with points in order of their significance. You can arrange points in either ascending or descending order of importance.

A useful, practical technique in preparing the main body of a presentation is to set aside a folder for each section and then assemble all relevant material you have into the respective folders.

Then, take each folder and sort the various references, notes, tables, quotes and other information you have assembled into an order in which you would like to discuss them. By having your material loose in folders, you can juggle the material around until you find it falling into a logical order and flow before you start writing.

The conclusion

You don't just stop once you have told the audience your key points, and you should not conclude just by thanking them or the organisers. A conclusion should do two important things.

1. It should summarise your main points. Tell 'em what you've told 'em. Recap your main points so the audience will remember them.

2. It should make a call to action. What do you want your audience to do? If it is a sales presentation, your conclusion should ask for the order. Alternatively, you may want your audience to vote on a policy, approve a proposal, go out on the street and protest, or vote for you in an election.

It is surprising how many people deliver a long presentation, with convincing points and exhaustive argument, and then fail to draw the presentation into a conclusion for the audience to take away and act on.

You can only deliver a winning presentation if you clearly and persuasively 'ask for the order'. Make sure your presentation has a summary of your main points in its conclusion and a clear summing up of what the audience should do.

It also helps if your conclusion has a climax at the end. This can be a memorable quote, a major statement, or a visual such as a video or slide.

The three parts of a presentation are overviewed in Figure 4.1.

How long should a presentation be?

There is no fixed rule on how long your presentation should be. But there is a considerable body of research which tells us how long people will sit in one room and listen attentively. You should tailor your presentation to how long people will listen—not to how long you want or need to talk.

'Many can rise to the occasion, but few know when to sit down' is a truism of presentations.

Franklin Roosevelt gave clear guidelines for the length of speeches when he said: 'Be sincere; be brief; be seated' (Stuart, 1988, p. 124).

Australians, renowned for their blunt Aussie humour, sum it up colloquially as: 'Stand up, speak up and shut up'.

As a general rule, most short presentations run between five and 10 minutes. Major reports and keynote addresses in conferences and annual general meetings usually run between 30 and 45 minutes. This is often too long. Most presenters would be better off cutting their presentations to, say, 20 minutes. They would probably still get the same amount of information across.

The video and audio-visual industry, which has undertaken considerable research to determine the ideal length of programs, has found that seven minutes should be the maximum length of most 'canned' presentations.

Outline plan and structure

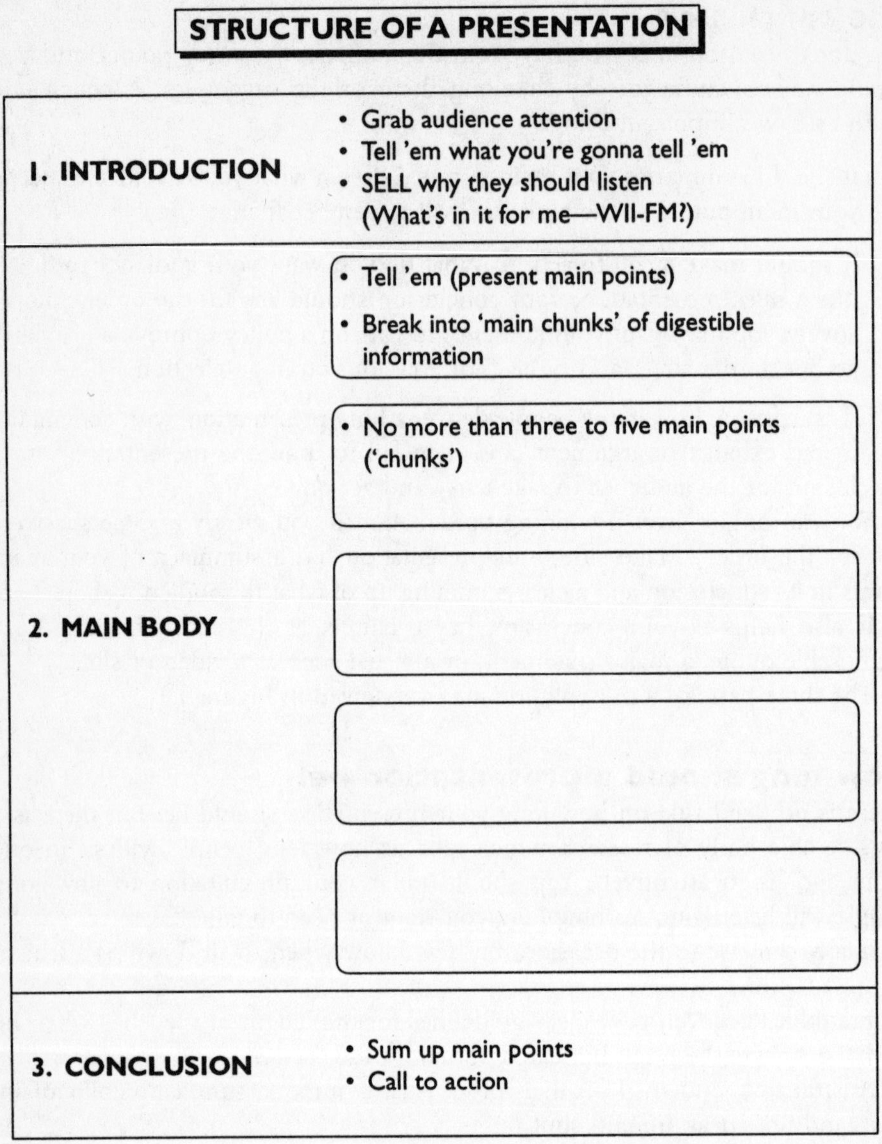

STRUCTURE OF A PRESENTATION

1. INTRODUCTION	• Grab audience attention • Tell 'em what you're gonna tell 'em • SELL why they should listen (What's in it for me—WII-FM?)
2. MAIN BODY	• Tell 'em (present main points) • Break into 'main chunks' of digestible information • No more than three to five main points ('chunks')
3. CONCLUSION	• Sum up main points • Call to action

FIGURE 4.1 *Structure of a presentation*

Ed McMahon, a well-known American TV presenter and speaker, said that 1,000 seconds was as long as most audiences would listen to a speaker. That's roughly 16.5 minutes (McMahon, 1986, pp. 22-24).

Figures 4.2 and 4.3 show how audience attention falls during various length presentations.

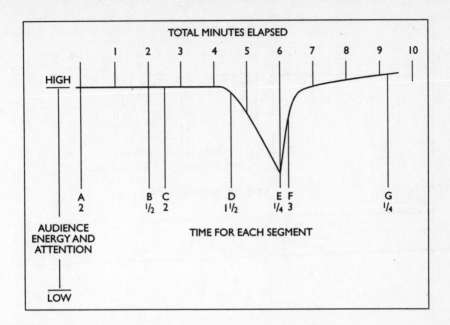

FIGURE 4.2 *Audience attention span in a 10 minute presentation*

Figure 4.2 shows that, during a 10 minute speech, audience attention starts to fall after just four or five minutes. After six or seven minutes, audience attention is in sharp decline unless something is done to restore interest.

Audience attention can be recovered by adding an interest point or 'refresher point'. This is an action or change of strategy by the presenter which recaptures audience attention. Interest or refresher points include introducing a new subject or issue, a visual such as a graph, chart or cartoon, an action or audience participation exercise.

Figure 4.3 demonstrates that several interest or refresher points are needed in a 20 minute presentation.

These diagrams dramatically illustrate the importance of carefully planning the main body of your presentation, including use of interest or refresher points. You need to grab the audience's attention back—to 'gather up the stragglers going down Route 350', as Christina Stuart says.

How to hold audience attention

Using a strong opening and having a clear structure in your presentation are critical to gaining and holding audience attention. But, as Figures 4.2 and 4.3 show, even with your best efforts, audience attention will decline and stray

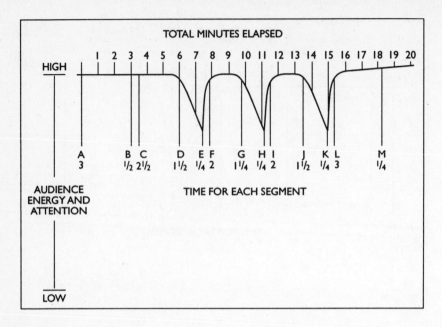

FIGURE 4.3 *Audience attention span in a 20 minute presentation*

without specific interest or refresher points. Refresher points which you can and should add to your presentation include:

○ asking a question of the audience;

○ asking a rhetorical question (even a rhetorical question makes people shuffle in their chairs and come back from Route 350 in case you ask them for an answer);

○ telling a story;

○ giving a demonstration;

○ telling a joke;

○ changing media (such as introducing overheads or slides);

○ showing a video;

○ conducting an exercise which involves audience participation.

Examine Figure 4.4 which shows the structure of a presentation again, this time with suggested refresher points marked. You will see the rationale for breaking your information into 'chunks' even more clearly now. The breaks between each chunk and the next are ideal times to insert a refresher point to

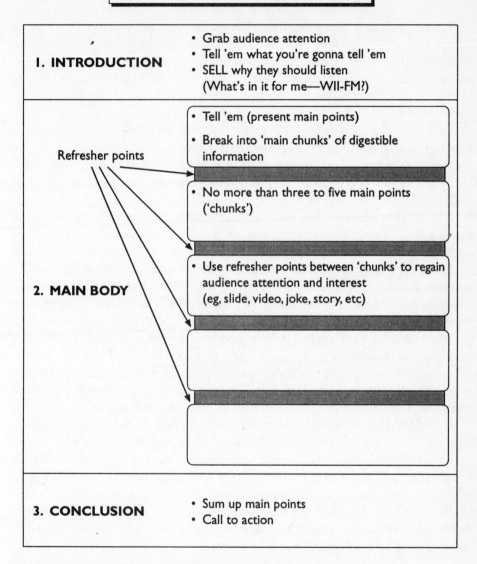

STRUCTURE OF A PRESENTATION

1. INTRODUCTION
- Grab audience attention
- Tell 'em what you're gonna tell 'em
- SELL why they should listen
  (What's in it for me—WII-FM?)

Refresher points

2. MAIN BODY
- Tell 'em (present main points)
- Break into 'main chunks' of digestible information

- No more than three to five main points ('chunks')

- Use refresher points between 'chunks' to regain audience attention and interest
  (eg, slide, video, joke, story, etc)

3. CONCLUSION
- Sum up main points
- Call to action

Outline plan and structure

FIGURE 4.4 *Structure of a presentation including refresher points*

rejuvenate audience interest and attention. These refresher points are the cement that glues your presentation together and gives it strength.

Refresher or interest points to regain audience attention do not always have to be between the chunks that comprise the main body of your presentation.

If you sense an audience's attention is straying, you can do something to regain audience interest any time during your presentation.

But you will find that unless you plan refresher points you will forget them. When you are in front of your audience delivering the main points of your presentation, you will be focused and will not have time to think about what you can do to respark interest. Also, adding in questions, audience participation, stories or jokes in the middle of a main point may interrupt the flow of your presentation.

So it is a good tip to add variations that will serve as refresher points in between your main chunks. This way, it is easier to remember them. But you must plan refresher points in the outline plan of your presentation or else, in the dynamics of delivery, you will forget them and lose your audience down Route 350.

Other techniques for adding interest and retaining audience attention will be discussed in later chapters, including some which will dramatically increase audience attention, retention and the impact of your presentations.

By now a picture should be emerging in your mind of a presentation which contains a number of elements—some of which you may not have thought about before. There is a lot more to a successful presentation than putting together information that you want to present on a particular topic.

You should spend time carefully constructing an outline plan of each presentation. This is your road map of where you want to go and how you want to get there. You have to plan each element of your presentation—the introduction, the chunks of your main body, the refresher points to regain and stimulate audience interest and attention during the presentation, and the conclusion.

In advance, you should plan any stories, jokes, audience exercises, demonstrations or other activities that will help you achieve the objectives of your presentation. This does not stifle spontaneity. Even the best comedians plan every aspect of their routines. You will need to plan these at outline stage to allow time for them in your presentation and to source the necessary material.

Having a clear structure will help you as a presenter in putting together and delivering your presentation. And it will help the audience in following you and remembering your information and messages.

Summary

O Structure your presentation with an opening, a main body and a conclusion. Use the 'Tell 'em' formula to remember this:

—Tell 'em what you're gonna tell 'em.
—Tell 'em.
—Tell 'em what you've told 'em.

○ Have an opening that grabs audience attention, tells 'em what you're gonna tell 'em, and whets their appetite about what's in it for them.

○ Break your main body up into 'chunks' of digestible information. Handle each chunk in four or five minutes.

○ Decide the order of presenting material in the main body—chronological, spatial, logical or topical (in order of importance).

○ Add interest or refresher points to recapture audience attention every four or five minutes. Ideally, you should plan refresher points between each chunk of information and the next, where you can tell a story, ask a question, use new aids such as slides or a video, etc.

○ Sum up your main points (Tell 'em what you've told 'em) and include a 'call to action' in your conclusion.

5

Research and assembly

When you know everything possible about your audience, your venue and have an outline plan of your presentation, you are still not ready to start writing your script or notes—not quite. There is one more important step before you put pen to paper or fingers to keyboard. You need to ensure that you have carried out adequate research and assembled sufficient material for the presentation you have planned.

It is critical that you complete an outline plan as discussed in Chapter 4 before starting this process, as it is only after you have a plan of what you will present that you can identify the ingredients that you will need. Even if you know your subject inside out, you may still need to carry out some research to come up with statistics, case studies, quotes, stories or anecdotes that will make your presentation really come together.

Importantly, research and assembly will include finding and assembling not only information for the main content of your presentation, but also any exercises, jokes, slides, videos or other elements that you decide on as refresher points.

If you undertake research and assembly of material for your presentation before preparing a detailed outline plan, you may finish up with too little material, or too much, material that does not fit together well, or you may neglect to collect information or aids which are necessary as refresher points.

On the other hand, if you have a detailed outline plan of your presentation, researching and assembling material will be a relatively quick process. You will not waste time gathering unnecessary information and you will be working with a clear idea of what you want—not just for yourself, but for your audience.

There are many simple, effective ways of researching and assembling material. Senior executives may have the resources of a department or public relations office to which they can delegate a large proportion of the 'leg work'.

Middle and junior executives and self-employed professionals are often on their own. However, there are a number of simple, effective research and preparation techniques available.

For instance, press clippings will often yield information or comments on your topic. Major newspapers maintain their own libraries (referred to in the trade as 'the morgue') where copies of all editions are kept and are available for public reference. Researching back copies is an effective way of gaining information about a topic. Better still, many major newspapers and magazines today provide the full text of current and back issues on CD-ROM allowing you to access vast amounts of information quickly and easily if you have access to a computer with a CD drive.

Also, in our electronic age, computer databases are available which allow instant research of specified subjects from a personal computer (PC). You can obtain company profiles, stock market information, government statistics and a wide range of other information either directly from special databases if you are a subscriber, or through on-line services such as CompuServe, Prodigy, America Online and the widely used Internet.

Computers will again be discussed in Chapter 6 'Writing your script or notes' and Chapter 7 'Presentation aids'. Using a computer can save a lot of time and help you research, assemble, write and deliver successful presentations.

A good bookshop or library may also have a number of books on your subject. Don't forget books which can provide general assistance, such as books of aphorisms, quotations, jokes and so on, as well as books specific to your topic or field of interest.

Another useful source of information about companies are their annual reports. As well, many companies and organisations publish corporate profiles which provide general information about their industries and operations. Many industries and professions publish a year book which is another quick and easy way to access information about particular sectors or fields.

Government census and statistics offices are an excellent source of national information and will usually provide information by phone, fax or, in some cases, by PC access.

Do as much research as possible. Don't start writing your presentation too early.

Being a bower bird

Many writers and successful presenters work in a constant cycle of research. Like the bower bird, which collects trinkets and odds and ends for its nest, they fossick for snippets of information, facts, interesting stories or anecdotes, case studies—even jokes that may suit a particular audience or situation. If you give presentations regularly, it is a good idea to become a 'bower bird' and start to collect materials that you may be able to use one day.

Of course, a good filing system will be essential, if you are to find things once you have filed them away.

Quotable quotes

Audiences respond to, and presentations are made more memorable by, interesting relevant quotes. We cannot all be a Plato or a Winston Churchill, but even President John F. Kennedy borrowed phrases and quotations from other people in many of his stirring and long-remembered speeches.

For instance, the famous lines 'Some people see things as they are and say "Why?" I dream things that never were, and say "Why not?"' are widely believed to have been Kennedy's own words. They were, in fact, written by Irish poet and author George Bernard Shaw and quoted by Kennedy.

Books of 'quotable quotes' and aphorisms are available in bookshops and libraries. These will give you a source of relevant and applicable quotes which you can select and use in presentations.

If you work on a PC, there are software programs available which provide quotations through an easy search facility. One such example, *The Colombia Dictionary of Quotations*, contains 18,000 famous and useful quotations which can be found in seconds.

Quotes can often provide that extra punch you are seeking to open a presentation or highlight a key point. Copyright should be acknowledged, but many anonymous quotes can be borrowed and built into a presentation. Here are just a few examples. When stuck for an opening, you could begin with:

> 'We all live under the same sky. But we don't all see the same horizon. Today, I want to talk about expanding our horizons in ...'

Quotes are often a way of adding a touch of humour, while still driving home a message. For instance:

> 'A pessimist is one who complains about the noise when opportunity knocks.'

Quotes can be pithy and meaningful. For example:

> 'Obstacles are what you see when you take your eyes off your goal.'

In trying to rally a group of staff or a team together, you could borrow the following quote:

> 'Snowflakes are such fragile things. But just look at what they become when they stick together.'

Don't overdo quotations. Used selectively, quotations can add a touch of class and memorability to your presentation. Good quotes move people's emotions.

However, avoid cliches—those quotations or sayings that have been worn out. For instance, every politician announcing an inquiry promises to 'leave no stone unturned'. The origin of this phrase was the Oracle at Delphi in Greek mythology of around 477 BC.

Stories and anecdotes

People enjoy stories, provided they are reasonably well told. Stories are a way of bringing a human element to a presentation and building empathy with your audience. The presenter who tells his or her audience: 'On the way here today I had an interesting experience ...' will immediately arouse their curiosity. Also, it gives an air of immediacy and spontaneity to your presentation—even if you prepared the story in advance.

On the other hand, stories which are long-winded and irrelevant take up valuable time. You should not tell long rambling stories. Any story that cannot be told in less then two minutes should not be used in a presentation.

A particular type of story or tale of an incident which emphasises a point you are making or which has special relevance is an anecdote. Here is a true story which was turned into an anecdote:

> Once I was due to give a presentation to a group of government public relations executives in Sydney. I had flown in from Hong Kong just the day before and had not fully unpacked.
>
> On the morning of my presentation, in my haste to dress—combined with a little jet lag—I accidentally put on one black shoe and one dark brown shoe. I did not notice my mistake until I was standing in the foyer of the hotel five minutes before the presentation. I can still feel that surge of panic when I looked down at my shoes for the first time.
>
> Acute embarrassment was my first reaction. There was no shoe shop nearby, so I had to find a way out of the situation. The audience was sure to notice as I am a 'walker'—I stroll around the stage when I talk.
>
> Then an idea came. Why not tell the story and use it for effect? My topic was 'Evaluation of Public Relations Programs' and I was trying to urge the audience which was a mix of academics and practitioners to reconcile theory and practice.

So I quickly restructured my opening and started by telling the story of how I came to be standing on the stage with one black shoe and one brown shoe. The audience had a good laugh with me and then I told them that this was the approach I would take and recommend to them in discussing evaluation—that they needed to stand with one foot in the academic world to understand theory, but with one foot in the practical world.

The presentation went well and the story worked so effectively that I brought it back into my conclusion. I summarised: 'So, just as I stand here today with one black shoe and one brown shoe, you need to stand with one foot firmly in the practical world, but with one in the academic world to apply more scientific methods and research rigour in measuring what you do in today's age of accountability.'

Jokes

Jokes are a fairway dotted with bunkers. You can make great progress using them, but there are major traps for the unwary and those who go off course. Like stories and anecdotes, jokes are most useful when they relate in some way to your presentation. For instance, if you are addressing an audience about economic issues, you could tell a joke about economists. For example:

> An economist died and made his way up to the Pearly Gates. St Peter looked at him and asked: 'What are you doing here?' The economist replied that he had died and he had come up to get into heaven. St Peter looked at him long and hard and said: 'All your life you have been predicting ups and downs and—guess what? You have got it wrong again.'

Most audiences of business people will laugh heartily at such a joke. But don't tell it to a group of economists unless you have the bravado to pull it off. This again illustrates the importance of audience analysis.

Likewise, beware of telling jokes about particular religions or cultures unless you are very sure you know your audience. And, in today's age of political correctness, and bearing in mind, of course, that you will no doubt have women in your audience, *never* tell sexist jokes.

Demonstrations

Some presentations lend themselves to a demonstration. For instance, a presentation on the benefits of using a computer for a particular application almost invariably needs to be demonstrated on a large screen. Describing in words what happens and how functions are carried out would be extremely difficult for an audience to follow.

Demonstrations can be used in a wide range of situations. To show how portable a device is, you could pass it around the audience and let people hold it. To show the handling characteristics of a new model car, you could stage the presentation outdoors at a track, or screen a short video. And so on.

A demonstration can also be used as a 'refresher point' to grab audience attention and refocus it on a particular point. For instance, in the mid 1980s I was invited to address an American Chamber of Commerce luncheon on marketing. AMCHAM luncheons are legendary, as presenters who do not measure up are pelted with bread rolls by the audience or 'gonged off' by the chairman.

I was apprehensive about holding the attention of such an audience for a presentation on marketing. So I decided on a demonstration to make a point about shotgun marketing versus targeted rifle shot marketing. As I approached the point of my presentation which referred to shotgun marketing, I leaned under the lectern and took out a shotgun which was loaded with a blank. I pointed it just over the heads of the audience and fired. As the smoke cleared, there were quite a few wide eyes and gaping mouths. I had their attention.

I remarked: 'See, with a shotgun approach I hit no one.' I then proceeded to espouse the benefits of carefully targeted, rifle shot marketing and, as I moved on to this topic, a soldier in full combat outfit ran on to the stage and crouched in a firing position with an automatic Armalite rifle.

'Be careful fingering those bread rolls,' I joked with growing confidence, feeling I had the complete attention of every person in the room.

Demonstrations can be as varied as you like. But they must be very carefully planned. Murphy's Law applies in demonstrations too: if things can go wrong, they will. A demonstration gone wrong can undermine your entire presentation. In my demonstration using a shotgun, I hired an armourer to load the right amount of gunpowder in the blank and supervise the exercise to ensure safety.

Audience participation

Although mostly used in training situations, audience participation can be used by any presenter to generate interest. It is very hard for people to nod off or daydream when they may be singled out at any moment and asked for a comment, response or some action.

On the other hand, many people don't like being put on the spot in front of others. Don't embarrass people with audience participation. Techniques used must suit the culture of the group. Americans are quite used to dynamic presentations that require the audience to stand up and even jump around doing exercises, whereas Asian audiences, for instance, are much more reticent and shy.

Importantly, audience participation must not be difficult. It must be fun— and should be relevant to your topic.

The simplest form of audience participation is asking questions of the audience and requesting either a show of hands or verbal responses. People generally like to have their opinion considered, so questions to the audience show you are interested in them and they get you involved with your audience. Questions stimulate a two-way flow of information which is what communication is all about.

Audience participation can also involve exercises such as asking your audience to complete a short quiz, nominate examples to support a point you are making, or even break into groups to discuss a topic.

Be careful, however, that audience participation exercises do not take you off the track and cause you to lose your flow or even lose control of the presentation. Every part of your presentation—including any stories or jokes you propose to tell, demonstrations or audience participation exercises—should be carefully prepared and any props required should be researched and assembled.

Ways to remember your presentation

A final point about researching and assembling your presentation is that you can make it much easier to remember and deliver if you assemble it with some thought and planning. There are a number of techniques which can help you remember the order as well as the content of your presentation.

○ *Numbered points*
The simplest method is to break your main body into 'chunks' numbered one, two, three, etc. You can 'signpost' this structure to your audience by saying, for instance: 'There are three key issues facing us that I would like to discuss today. The first is...'

○ *Mnemonics*
You can increase both your audience's and your ability to remember key points using mnemonics. Mnemonics help us remember things through sound association. For instance, if you are training a group in how to write proposals, you could structure your presentation around 'five Ps' these being:

—Preface (the introduction);
—Position (where we are currently);
—Problem (what we have to overcome or address);
—Plan (what we are going to do about it);
—Postscript (conclusions and implementation).

Most audiences will remember 'the five Ps' long after other training lectures or presentations are forgotten.

○ *Acronyms*

Another way to increase your audience's and your ability to remember a presentation is to arrange key points with the first letter forming a word that can be easily recalled.

For instance, a company committed to customer service helped its staff remember this by creating as its theme 'Customers Are the Reason for our Existence' which was abbreviated to CARE.

Chapter 9 of this handbook, which discusses delivery of presentations, uses an acronym, SOFTEN, to help you remember the main points of body language:

S   Smile;
O   Open stance;
F   Forward lean;
T   Tone;
E   Eye contact;
N   Nod.

It is not always possible to create an acronym or use mnemonics. Creating strained acronyms affords little benefit. But consider whether you can make your presentation more memorable and logically ordered when you are assembling your material. Careful research and assembly can make a big difference to the final delivery of your presentation.

Summary

○ Once you have an outline plan of your presentation, carry out research and assemble material to ensure you have all the information and resources you need.

○ As well as information about your topic, you will need to research and assemble stories, anecdotes, jokes, exercises or demonstrations that you have planned as part of your main content or as 'refresher points'.

○ Be a 'bower bird' and continually collect interesting and useful material for presentations.

○ Access newspaper and magazine clippings either in hard copy or using CD-ROM, books, annual reports, corporate profiles, directories, government statistics, databases and on-line services as sources of information.

○ Plan how you can make your structure easy to remember using techniques such as numbered points or acronyms that represent your key points.

6

*Writing your script
or notes*

At last, you say! Finally we can write a presentation. This is where many would-be presenters begin and we are only just getting to it after five chapters.

Lest you feel the first five chapters are wasting time and you can begin at this point, remember the iceberg analogy. Three-quarters or even more of a successful presentation lie below the surface like an iceberg. Without that base, the peak that we see above the surface will topple and sink. So it is with presentations.

If you have carefully carried out audience analysis, venue reconnaissance, prepared an outline plan and a structure for what you are going to say and do, and then researched and assembled the material needed, you will be able to write your presentation in no time at all. Writing your script or notes is simply joining up all the pieces you have prepared in the order set out in your outline plan. And you know your outline plan will work because you developed it taking into account your audience and the venue at which you are going to present.

Writing a report, plan, novel or a presentation is slow and difficult if you do not have a clear idea of your audience and a clear plan to work to. While writing may never be easy for you, it is much easier and quicker when you have done your groundwork.

When you sit down to write your script or notes, have the outline plan of your presentation in front of you. Draw it up on a flip chart or a large sheet of paper if you wish. The clearer the road map and your directions, the quicker you will be able to get to your destination.

You may have noticed use of the terms 'script' or notes, rather than 'speech'. A script may appear to relate more to a movie or play rather than to giving presentations. However, the choice of word is deliberate.

As explained at the beginning, presentations are more than speaking. Presentations can, and frequently do, involve visual aids, audience involvement, demonstrations, exercises, questions, etc. These activities, as well as the words you plan to say, should be scripted for your presentation. So 'script' is an appropriate term. Alternatively, you may wish to speak from notes depending on the type of presentation you plan to give.

Four types of presentations

In sitting down to write a script or notes for a presentation, the first question that arises is what kind of presentation are you going to give?

There are four basic types of speeches or presentations. Although different terms may be used in some places, the main speech formats are:

1. *Impromptu*
    An impromptu speech or presentation is completely off-the-cuff with little or no time to prepare.

2. *Memorised*
    As the name suggests, a memorised speech is written in full and then completely memorised. Memorisation of speeches or presentations is difficult if not impossible, so you can forget this one from the outset.

3. *Read*
    A very common type of speech—unfortunately. Speeches which are written in full and then read are almost always boring, as the presenter is constantly looking down at his or her text and usually can do no more than read. So read speeches tend to be just that—speeches, not presentations.

4. *Prepared and delivered from notes or cue cards*
    The fourth type of presentation is one which is fully prepared, even to a complete script in some cases, but then delivered from notes or cue cards in a natural non-read way. This type is also called an extemporaneous presentation.

Presentations in business and professional fields almost always fall into the third or fourth categories. Impromptu speeches usually only apply to social functions or for very short addresses such as moving a vote of thanks or supporting a motion at a meeting. And memorisation is only applicable if you are an actor trained in learning lines.

Furthermore, read speeches are discouraged by most communication consultants and speaker trainers. Some senior executives persist with them under the illusion that their message is getting across. Research shows low audience interest, retention and impact from read presentations.

By far the most popular presentations in business and professional fields are those that are prepared in great detail and then delivered in a natural way using notes, cue cards or other aids to help the presenter and the audience.

Don't be fooled by impressions that these kind of presentations come naturally to certain presenters. Even though some may make it look easy and natural, successful presentations come no more naturally than pin-point serves come to a tennis ace or triple somersaults come to a gymnast. They are the result of lots of training and hard work. But the more work done at the beginning, the easier it will be on the day—or the night.

With the magic of new technology, there is one variation on read presentations that is acceptable to certain audiences. If the equipment is available, presenters can use a teleprompter similar to those used by television news readers. This is a special word processing system that projects the script into one or more small glass reflector panels mounted on stands in front of the presenter. A teleprompter operator scrolls the script at the right speed for the presenter on the glass reflectors which are almost unnoticeable to the audience. This way, a presenter can read his or her script, but appears to be looking at the audience. If several reflectors are used—say, one left and one right—the presenter can alternate between them and appear to be scanning across both sides of the audience.

It is unlikely you will use a teleprompter for most presentations. If you do, there is more information on teleprompters in Chapter 7 'Presentation aids'.

In most cases, you should plan to give a well-prepared presentation based on a detailed script, summarised into notes, cue cards or other aids for use as delivery prompts.

Script or notes?

Most presenters will find it necessary and advantageous to write their presentation out in full at least once. Even if you end up delivering the presentation from notes or cue cards, writing it out helps to distil your thoughts and to develop your ideas.

If you have access to a word processor, this will save considerable time as any good speech will go through several rewrites and lots of editing and polishing.

Whether to use notes, cue cards or some other form of prompt when delivering your presentation will be discussed at the end of this chapter after you have prepared your script in full.

Writing style

An important, practical rule in preparing a script for a presentation is: 'Don't write, speak'. Do not write a presentation the way you write reports or proposals. In general, presentation scripts will have shorter sentences than written texts, as an audience cannot go back and re-read a sentence if they are not sure of its meaning. A presentation script does not need to strictly follow rules of grammar. For instance, while we are taught that every sentence must have a verb, effect can be created in a presentation by using short, stabbing phrases and bullet points which are not complete sentences.

Don't use very long words and long sentences. You will find that you will stumble over them, or run out of breath when delivering them.

It is important to vary the length of sentences when writing your script. Sentences of equal length sound monotonous. Speak your script out loud to hear how it sounds.

The most important rule of all is to write your script the way you talk. It should be natural. Don't be afraid to use colloquial words and phrases if these are the vernacular of the audience. The art of script writing is clarity and smoothness, natural flow—not flowery prose and impressive pontification.

Don't, for instance, use this kind of mumbo-jumbo which was taken from a speech to staff by the administrator of a superannuation fund:

> Circumstances occasionally arise involving a situation in which one or more of the contributing personnel wishes to exercise the option of continuing in employment beyond the normal retirement date as specified in their formal contractual agreement; in which eventuality suitable arrangements can be concluded for the further maintenance of contribution and consequent enhancement of eventual benefit.

The above presenter could simply have said: 'Sometimes people want to continue working after they turn 60. If they do, they can stay in the pension plan.'

Title of your presentation

All presentations begin with a title—although you don't necessarily have to write the title first. In fact, it is often preferable to leave your title till last. Unless something obvious springs to mind, a title will come to you much more easily when you have the whole presentation in front of you.

Select a catchy, interesting or even controversial title for your presentation. Too many presenters choose obvious, boring titles. Rather than entitling your presentation, 'Planning and Implementing a Productivity Scheme in XYZ Corporation', you could call your presentation 'Putting XYZ Corporation Among the Bulls'. Instead of 'Trends in the PC Industry in the 1990s', you could create a title such as 'Computers—Big Brother or Little Helper in the 90s'. One of my favourite presentations is to senior executives on the importance of media interview training which I title 'How To Make or Break Your Company and Career in 30 Seconds'.

Creative and different titles evoke interest and speculation among the audience. A title should titillate the audience, while being relevant and not over-promising.

Typing your script or notes

From your audience analysis and venue reconnaissance, you will know in advance whether a copy of your presentation is to be handed out to the audience, or possibly distributed to others such as the media. If a hard copy is to be handed out, you will need two versions of your presentation:

1. full text;

2. script, notes or cue cards for delivery.

The full text of your presentation can be word processed in the normal manner—that is, in standard type fonts, single spaced on quarto or international A4 size paper. However, your delivery script or notes will differ in a number of ways.

First, if you are going to read your presentation, you will not easily be able to read standard size typefaces in single line spacing when you are standing at a lectern or with your script in your hand in front of an audience. A delivery version of your script should be printed in 16 or 18 point type (most office type is 12 point) with one and a half or double spacing.

Each presenter has his or her own preferences. But the most legible types are serif (with the squiggles on the ends of the letters) in capitals and lower case. Type in all capitals is harder to read.

This is a sample of 18 point Times New Roman with extra spacing:

Ladies and gentlemen. Today I would like to introduce you to our company's new superannuation plan which will mean many thousands of dollars to you and security for your future.

Secondly, your delivery script will need notations or instructions for yourself—such as when to show slides or when to tell a story. You will not want these comments to appear in a printed version of your presentation.

Thirdly, if you have accepted that you should not read your presentation, then you will need to highlight parts of your script in some way. Some presenters use a highlight pen to mark key sections and then refer to these at various intervals during their presentation. Others like to write notes and instructions for themselves all over the delivery copy of their presentation.

Better still, you should retype shorter notes for yourself which encapsulate the main headings and key points of your presentation to serve as memory joggers. If you know your presentation well, these brief points will be sufficient to remind you of what you want to present.

Some presenters like to have these notes mounted or written on cards which they can hold unobtrusively in their hands while presenting. Or you may be comfortable typing your notes on sheets of paper and placing these on the lectern.

A number of modern presentation software packages have a provision for speaker's notes to be typed directly under overheads of slides generated on a personal computer. These provide excellent speaker's notes and will be further discussed in Chapter 7.

Tips on when to distribute copies of your presentation will be further discussed under 'Handouts' in Chapter 10.

Summary

O Prepare your presentation script in full, but then work from notes. Don't read your script verbatim. And don't try to memorise it.

O Don't write a presentation, speak it. Practise your script out loud while you are preparing it. Use a natural style of spoken language—not prose or pontification.

O Type your notes or delivery version of your script in large letters which can be easily read.

O Leave your title till the end. It will be easier and you will write a better title when you have the whole presentation in front of you.

Presentation aids

This is one of the most important chapters in this book. Read it at least twice.

There are two compelling reasons for considering presentation aids in detail. First, in today's technological age, it is inevitable that presenters will come up against equipment discussed in this chapter. Sooner or later, whether you like it or not, you will find yourself confronted and confused by a lectern that looks like the flight deck of the space shuttle, whiteboards that operate electronically and seem to have a mind of their own, PA systems that have you wired for sound like a rock star, or infra-red remote controls that confuse you more than your VCR.

Secondly, this chapter explains a range of aids which, when understood and used effectively, can make your job as a presenter much easier and can dramatically improve the impact, professionalism and retention of your presentations.

This chapter explains traditional aids such as overhead transparencies and whiteboards and will introduce you to modern presentation technologies such as PC presentations and multimedia which are increasingly being used by progressive corporations, organisations, training institutions and conference organisers.

If you understand and use these aids effectively, they can be powerful tools to help you deliver successful presentations.

Visual support

Many presenters have an outdated and negative view of visual presentation aids. This is largely because of experiences with equipment in the past—projectors that broke down or did not work, blown bulbs, poor quality images on screen and systems that were difficult to operate.

Information about visual presentation in many books is also largely out of date, having been overtaken by rapid changes in technology. For instance, Ed Wohlmuth's widely used text, *The Overnight Guide to Public Speaking* (Wohlmuth, 1983, p. 129) says: 'Visuals are almost always cumbersome, slowing the pace of the presentation far below what's required for complete audience involvement.'

Another book, still widely marketed as a speaker's guide, advises presenters to sit beside an overhead projector so they can write on it as they speak (Stuart, 1988, p. 142). One of the world's most influential speakers, Edward de Bono, uses this technique. But for most presenters, sitting and writing on overhead transparencies as they speak is likely to result in chicken scrawl visuals and bored audiences.

Niki Flacks and Robert Rasberry, in their book *Power Talk*, reflect the age-old fears of many presenters with their comments on visuals (Flacks & Rasberry, 1982, p. 130). They warn:

O   they can steal the show from you;

O   they are hard to work with and are especially hard to coordinate smoothly into a speech;

O   they are time-consuming to construct;

O   they can be anxiety-provoking, especially if they involve electrical equipment that sometimes does not work properly;

O   they can be boring if over-used.

Most of these claims are nonsense. You are the presenter, in control of the presentation. If you know what you are doing, your visuals will only appear when you want them to and say what you want them to say.

While modern presentation equipment is not infallible, systems have changed radically. Most equipment used today is highly reliable, simple to operate and very effective. Careful preparation, venue reconnaissance and a little familiarisation training of presenters can reduce risks to a negligible level.

With graphics programs widely available on personal computers and high quality overhead transparencies able to be made on laser or colour printers available in most offices these days, one can hardly sustain an argument that visuals are difficult to make. The days of Letraset and adhesive tape are gone.

And, far from interrupting your presentation, visuals can actually help you maintain your flow and rhythm. Automatically changed visuals, such as slides in a carousel projector system, allow you to speak without interruption.

Furthermore, while the purists argue that a presenter should not look at the screen, visual aids provide an anxiety-reducing safety net for you. Certainly, you should not read your presentation off the screen as a general rule. But when you are up there in front of the audience, it is comforting to know that the main points of your presentation are shown in order on your visual aids. If you lose your place or can't think what comes next, you can always sneak a glance at your visuals.

Most importantly, visuals can add to the effectiveness of your presentation. In many instances, visual reinforcement of your presentation is essential for effective communication.

Doug Malouf, in *How to Create and Deliver a Dynamic Presentation*, gives the dramatic comparison of reception through our five senses (Malouf, 1988, p. 81):

○ Smell   3%

○ Taste   4%

○ Touch   7%

○ Hearing   11%

○ Sight   75%

Figure 7.1 shows the relative impact of voice, words and visual communication on an audience. A study from the University of California at Los Angeles (UCLA) found more than 90% of what an audience understands and believes comes from visual and audio messages. Text accounts for only 7% (Brody & Kent, 1993, p. 23).

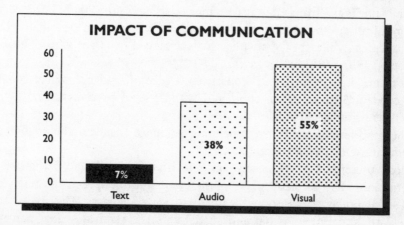

FIGURE 7.1 *The impact of text, audio and visual communication*

A study by the influential Wharton Research Center at the University of Pennsylvania in 1981 found that retention of verbal only presentations is just 10%. By comparison, the retention rate of combined verbal and visual communication is 50%—a 400% increase in effectiveness (Hallan, 1993, pp. 42-43).

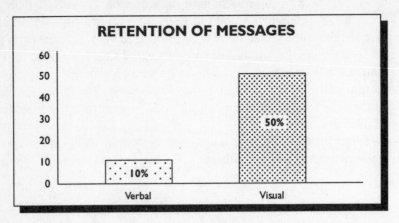

FIGURE 7.2 *Retention of verbal and visual messages*
(Source: Wharton study, US)

The power of visual communication is further borne out by a 1986 study sponsored by 3M and conducted by the University of Minnesota Management Information Systems Research Center which confirmed the conclusions of the Wharton study and found presenters who used computer generated slides and overhead transparencies were 43% more persuasive than presenters who did not use visuals (Hallan, 1993, p. 43).

A report published by Decker Communications Inc. in the US produced similar findings from its research as shown in Figure 7.3. Decker Communications found that speakers without visuals achieved their goals in 33% of cases, while speakers with visuals achieved their goals in 67% of cases (Malouf, 1988, p. 82).

In terms of reaching group consensus, Decker found non-visual presenters succeeded in 58% of cases, compared with 79% of presenters who achieved consensus using visual aids.

These findings provide overwhelming evidence that you should use visual communication in your presentations.

Most presenters rely heavily on left brain thinking to structure their presentations. The left hemisphere of the brain controls speech and many of the intellectual processes associated with logic and language. 'The right brain is particularly superior in visual and spatial abilities, such as spatial perception, musical abilities, tactile sensations, intuitive feelings and perceptual insight,' say

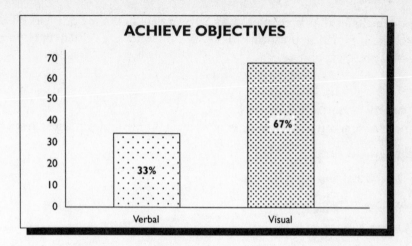

FIGURE 7.3   *Achievement of objectives through verbal and visual communication*
(Source: Decker Communications)

Niki Flacks and Robert Rasberry in their popular *Power Talk* program (Flacks & Rasberry, 1982, p. 12). You should try to balance left and right brain thinking in your presentations.

When used effectively, not only can visual presentations get your message across with better results; they can save you time and money. For instance, visual communication can reduce the time taken to present important information. Research by the University of Minnesota in 1986 found the average length of meetings when visual aids were not used was 26.7 minutes. When visuals were used, average meeting length reduced to 18.6 minutes—a saving of 28% in executive time.

With executive time worth anywhere from $100 to $300 an hour, pictures can not only be effective in communicating a thousand words. A picture can be worth a thousand dollars!

Despite the proven benefits, a 1989 study conducted by the Annenberg School of Communications at the University of Southern California, Los Angeles, found a majority of business meetings are convened without any visual aids.

When visuals are used, the standard is often very poor. Many trainers and executives insist on using only the most primitive visual aids, including typewritten or handwritten overhead transparencies that are barely readable from the first row with a pair of binoculars. Presentations in which slides or overheads are shown upside down or back-to-front are all too common. And whole pages of text or columns of figures are often taken directly from a written report and put on overheads or slides, making them cluttered and confusing.

The remainder of this chapter gives an overview of the major types of visual support and provides practical advice on how to use visual aids to give successful presentations.

Types of visual support

The most common types of visual communication media for presentations are:

O   flip charts;

O   whiteboards and blackboards;

O   electronic whiteboards;

O   overhead transparencies;

O   35mm slides;

O   video;

O   personal computers (PCs) linked to overhead projectors, LCD panels or data projectors.

Visual aids can be comprised of graphics, photographs, or they can be composites. Examples of graphics include:

O   pie, column, bar and line charts;

O   graphs;

O   organisation charts;

O   diagrams and drawings;

O   tables;

O   key words or text;

O   cartoons.

Photographs include such things as products, locations and people.
Examples of composites include:

O   photographic scenes with graphic information inserted (eg, a photograph of a facility such as a manufacturing plant with a graph or table of production levels);

O   graphics, such as an organisational chart with photographs of key people dropped in;

O   product shots with graphic enhancement.

Whiteboards and blackboards

Whiteboards are now more popular than blackboards in most sectors. They are effective communication tools for small groups, such as in a workshop or boardroom situation with a very small audience.

If your presentation revolves more around discussion than formal presentation, you may not be able to prepare visuals in advance. A whiteboard gives you the flexibility to write key words or draw diagrams, flow charts and so on while you are presenting, or in response to discussion.

Advantages

O   flexibility—you can decide at the time what to write;

O   corrections can be made easily—you can simply rub out information;

O   no cost;

O   ability to put the audience's points on to the screen as well as yours.

Disadvantages

O   legibility is limited by your handwriting;

O   your back is to the audience when you are writing;

O   you cannot write and talk at the same time, so flow and rhythm are interrupted;

O   your visuals are not portable (that is, they cannot be taken to another presentation);

O   you usually have only a single whiteboard and once the board is full you have to erase information;

O   pens or chalk are messy. Felt pens, in particular, frequently dry out when tops are left off;

O   ineffective for audiences of more than 10-15.

CHECKLIST FOR USING WHITEBOARDS

O   **Check pens before you start** to ensure they work.

O   **Write or draw neatly and large enough** so the whole audience can read your visuals.

continued ...

O Write your text and then **turn to face the audience before speaking**. Your voice may be lost if you talk facing the board, and research shows that people listen less when there is no eye contact.

O **Put the caps back on pens** whenever you stop writing, as they dry out quickly.

O **Rub out information no longer needed** to avoid distractions and clutter.

O **Avoid squeaking caused by felt pens.** This is very disconcerting to audiences.

O **Use a more modern and efficient type of visual support** if possible.

Flip charts

Flip charts use large sheets of paper mounted on an easel. As you finish writing on each sheet with a felt pen, you can tear it off or flip it back over the stand to move to the next one. Flip charts are similar to whiteboards, but have some additional benefits. However, you should also carefully note the disadvantages of flip charts.

Advantages

O flexibility—you can decide at the time what to write;

O better than whiteboards in that you can prepare them before your presentation or meeting;

O you can return to a previous sheet if you need to go back to a point, or tear them off and stick them on the wall for later reference;

O you can retain them afterwards—you may take them back to your office for typing up as notes;

O low cost;

O available almost anywhere.

Disadvantages

O legibility is limited by your handwriting;

O your back is to the audience when you are writing;

O you cannot write and talk at the same time, so flow and rhythm are interrupted;

○ low quality paper and felt pens can be messy;

○ limited portability as flip charts are usually not suitable to take to more than one meeting;

○ noisy and distracting when changing sheets;

○ not suitable for audiences of more than 15-20.

CHECKLIST FOR USING FLIP CHARTS

○ **Site the easel high enough** so that people at the back can see. Most flip chart easels have adjustable legs.

○ **Check pens before you start** to ensure they work.

○ **Write or draw neatly and large enough** so the whole audience can read your visuals.

○ Write your text and then **turn to face the audience before speaking**. Your voice may be lost if you talk facing the board, and research shows that people listen less when there is no eye contact.

○ **Put the caps back on pens** whenever you stop writing, as they dry out quickly.

○ **Fold back or tear off completed sheets** so they don't distract the audience.

○ **Minimise rustling of paper** when you turn over or tear off sheets of paper. Flip charts can be quite noisy and distracting to an audience.

○ **Use a more modern and efficient type of visual support** if possible.

Electronic whiteboards

Electronic whiteboards have been developed offering major advantages over their traditional namesakes, and are now in use in many offices, conference and training rooms.

Electronic whiteboards have an electric motor which scrolls the screen to expose a new clean section once one section of the whiteboard is full. Most importantly, electronic whiteboard screens are connected to a small printer which can, at the touch of a button, provide print-outs of what you write on the screen. This allows you to retain or distribute copies of what you have discussed in a meeting, workshop or seminar.

Electronic whiteboards are very effective for small discussion groups and meetings, but are generally unsuitable for large groups because they suffer from many of the same disadvantages as traditional whiteboards and flip charts.

Advantages

○ flexibility—you can decide at the time what to write;

○ corrections can be made easily—you can simply rub out information;

○ no cost (provided they are available at the venue);

○ ability to put the audience's points on to the screen as well as yours;

○ better than traditional whiteboards and flip charts as print-outs of information can be retained or circulated.

Disadvantages

○ legibility is limited by your handwriting;

○ your back is to the audience when you are writing;

○ you cannot write and talk at the same time, so flow and rhythm are interrupted;

○ print-outs are often low quality and hard to read because of poor handwriting;

○ many presenters have trouble using them. Without familiarisation, an electronic whiteboard will end up entertaining the audience and embarrassing the presenter with its whirrings and random scrolling as the presenter fumbles with the controls.

CHECKLIST FOR USING ELECTRONIC WHITEBOARDS

Most of the same guidelines applying to standard whiteboards also apply to electronic whiteboards. In addition, you should:

○ **Familiarise yourself with the controls** before using an electronic whiteboard. A few minutes practising and learning which buttons do what will make your presentation go much more smoothly.

continued ...

○ **Ensure the printer is working** if you wish to obtain print-outs of your work.

○ **Write in dark colours only**—black, brown or dark blue—not in pastels, as these will not print out clearly.

○ **Ensure you rub out any confidential information**—including what has been scrolled behind the facing section. It is easy to forget important information once it is out of sight. Many industrial espionage experts say that leaks are often as simple as someone scrolling back through electronic whiteboards to read information left after a meeting.

Overhead transparencies

Surveys indicate that overhead transparencies are still the most popular form of visual support used by presenters, although this is changing.

The first annual presentation graphics survey conducted by the Genigraphics Corporation in 1987 gave an illuminating insight into business presentations in the US. Similar trends have been observed in the UK, Europe and other countries, including Australia and Canada. The Genigraphics survey found that 57% of overheads are produced on a photocopier and that, most often, these are made from typewritten or even handwritten text (Macnamara & Venton, 1990, pp. 56-57).

Typewritten letters and numbers are too thin to project clearly onto a screen. Usually, the size of typewritten text is also too small for projection. And the less said about handwritten overhead transparencies the better!

Only 29% of overheads were made from artwork and 32% from computer graphics at the time of the Genigraphics survey. However, with the enormous increase in use of personal computers in offices and homes, the number made from computer graphics is growing rapidly. With PCs and the easy-to-use graphics programs now available, high quality graphs, charts, diagrams and text overheads can be made cost-efficiently.

You should note the following advantages and disadvantages of overhead transparencies.

Advantages

○ quick and cheap to produce if made on a photocopier or laser printer available in most offices;

○ can also be made in high quality, full colour from artwork or by computer graphics (but more expensive);

○ screen is bright and clear even in fully lit rooms;

○ the order of your visuals can be quickly and easily changed even moments before your presentation;

○ information can be revealed progressively, but this has to be done manually with overlays or moving a piece of paper to uncover text;

○ overhead projectors are available in almost all offices, conference and training facilities worldwide.

Disadvantages

○ poor quality when made from handwritten or typewritten text;

○ usually black and white only when produced on a photocopier;

○ allow light on the screen when not framed;

○ have to be changed manually which breaks the presenter's flow and distracts the audience;

○ most overhead projectors suffer from keystoning (distortion of the image caused by the projector being too low or at an angle to the screen);

○ the overhead projector has to be positioned directly in front of the screen and may block the view of part of the audience;

○ the fan in overhead projectors is often noisy and may run for cooling even when the lamp is not on;

○ projectors have to be turned on and off to avoid leaving irrelevant information on the screen;

○ transparencies are sensitive to fingerprints and easily damaged.

CHECKLIST FOR USING OVERHEADS

○ Make sure **the projector is lined up at 90 degrees to the screen and low** so it does not block the audience's view. However, if the projector is too low, you will see distortion on the screen, called keystoning. To avoid keystoning:

○ Ensure the **screen is at least 1.2 metres above the floor** and the **projector is 0.75 to one metre above the floor.**

continued ...

O Note that most portable screens have a **keystone eliminator**—a small extender arm that allows the top of the screen to be tilted forward to straighten the angle and eliminate or reduce distortion. If ordering a portable screen for overhead projection, request a keystone eliminator. That will really impress the locals!

O Have the **audience at no more than a 45 degree angle to the screen**. Any sharper angle and they won't see your visuals clearly.

O Produce **quality overheads from artwork or computer graphics**. Desktop publishing typesetting is acceptable. **Do not use overheads from typewritten text or handwriting** for major presentations.

O **Use clean large type for legibility** (say 18 or 20 point Arial or Helvetica type). Don't use typefaces with thin serifs as these don't project well.

O Use **no more than five or six words per line** and no more than **five to seven lines per overhead**. There are no fixed rules, but use common sense and follow John Cleese's pertinent summary: 'Use as many words as you would on a T-shirt'.

O **Keep your overheads simple and uncluttered**, especially when trying out new computer graphics programs, and avoid over-doing graphs and charts. Beware of what data presentation researcher, Edward Tufte, calls 'chartjunk'.

O **Never produce overhead transparencies directly from full pages of text or figures**. If you do, no one will be able to read your overheads.

O **Don't project off the screen** on to the walls or ceiling. Adjust the projector to screen distance.

O **Turn the projector off before removing or placing a transparency** to avoid the distraction of information sliding across the screen.

O **Have someone change your overheads** if possible to prevent interruption to your presentation.

O **Don't black-out or brown-out the room**. Most overhead projectors work fine in a fully lit room. **Dim lights slightly** if dimming facilities are available.

O **Avoid lights shining directly on the screen** as this will white-out your image.

continued ...

○ If possible, **mount overhead transparencies in frames**. This allows numbering to keep them in order and eliminates unwanted light around the edges of the screen .

○ **Remove static electricity from your overheads** which causes them to stick together. You can do this simply by rubbing your overheads together gently, or by putting them together and pulling them apart several times before use.

○ **Clean the glass top of the overhead projector thoroughly before use.** Specks of dust and marks will project on your overheads.

○ Try to pace your overheads at **one every 40 to 80 seconds.**

○ **Don't leave overheads on screen when they are no longer relevant.**

○ **Don't stand in front of the projector.**

○ **Don't point with you hand**—it will appear as a large black blob on the screen. Use a fine pencil or pointer on the transparency; do not point it at the screen.

○ **Don't hand write on overheads** when using them. Unless you are a calligrapher, the result is messy and interrupts your presentation.

○ **Talk to the audience; don't look at the screen.**

○ **Reveal points one by one using a mask**, not all together, as the audience will be reading ahead and not listening to you.

○ **Turn off the lamp** when you are not using overheads.

○ **Store your overhead transparencies carefully**. Even fine scratches will ruin your presentation.

Use these major checklists when preparing your presentations. Copyright is granted to make copies for your own use (but not for distribution).

Slides

During the 1980s, slides became one of the most popular forms of visual presentations and are still used widely for a number of reasons. Slides can be photographic, graphics, or composites of the two, so they have wide application in presentations.

Because slides use 35mm film, the same format as theatre-release movies, they project very high quality images. As well, they are small and can be easily transported. For instance, an entire presentation of slides can be carried in a briefcase or a small carousel ready for projection.

While photographic slides continue to be widely used, the major influence on visual presentations has been the evolution of computer graphics for slide production. Computer graphic slides can be made with very high resolution and up to 16 million colour shades, giving very sharp, high impact presentations on screen. They are also relatively quick to produce.

Another key advantage of computer graphics is that text, graphs, charts, tables, diagrams and even animation created on graphic slides can be stored on computer disk. This means that they can be kept for future use, easily updated if necessary, or enhanced at a later stage for a new presentation.

Two main options are available for presenters wanting to produce quality graphic or composite slides. You can either:

1. commission a specialist computer graphics bureau to custom design and produce the slides for you; or

2. create the slides in-house on a PC and then have the digital information transferred on to 35mm film by a bureau (called 'imaging'). The output device to reproduce slides from computer disk on to 35mm film is a film recorder and these are usually not found in most companies and organisations.

A number of popular graphics and specialist presentations software programs are available for both industry standard (IBM type) PCs and Apple Macintosh computers. These will be further discussed under 'PC Presentations' later in this chapter.

In most major cities around the world, there are production houses or bureaux which can either fully produce slides for you, or image your PC graphics onto slides. Imaging and mounting of simple computer generated slides costs between $10 and $20 per slide, while fully custom-designed slides can cost from $50 to several hundred dollars each depending on your requirements.

Note the following major advantages and disadvantages of 35mm slides.

Advantages

O photographic colour slides can be easily made by anyone with a simple camera;

○ high quality graphic slides with 4,000 line resolution and up to 16 million colour shades can be produced using a PC, or by commissioning a specialist bureau or production house;

○ composite slides can be made merging photographic and graphic information;

○ high creativity is available, including 3D and special effects if a graphic designer is used;

○ durability—when mounted in strong frames under glass;

○ well-protected from fingerprints and damage when mounted under glass;

○ easily portable when loaded into a carousel;

○ computer generated slides can be stored on disk for filing and for easy updating;

○ hard copy print-outs can be made easily on a laser printer when slides are produced on a PC;

○ slide projectors are usually smaller and more portable than most overhead projectors.

Disadvantages

○ they usually require at least three to four days for production if a bureau or production house is used;

○ relatively costly (from $10–$20 for imaging of your computer generated slides, or from $50 up to several hundred dollars for complete design and production by a specialist bureau or production house).

CHECKLIST FOR USING SLIDES

○ Make sure 35mm slides are mounted in **strong plastic or metal frames** that will not crack or separate—not paper mounts.

○ Have your presentation slides **glass-mounted** to prevent 'popping' under the heat of the projector lamp (celluloid film expands and bends under heat which sends the image out of focus).

continued ...

○ **Do not mix mounted and unmounted slides or different thickness mounts** as this will vary the focus of your projected image.

○ **Check that all slides are wiped clean** of fingerprints and dust before projecting. Even hairs and particles of dust will appear as thick lines or spots on the screen.

○ Select **a colour combination, background and a layout** for slides in your presentation. Different colours can be used for different sections or points, or bright new colours can be introduced to add audience interest. But don't go overboard with colour. Select a clean, uncluttered design format.

○ Use **contrasting colours that are easily readable for text** (eg, yellow text on a dark blue background or white against blue) and/or shadow letters to highlight text against the background where softer colours are used. In choosing your colour scheme, note that psychologists tell us that:

—grey implies quiet, conservative and stable;

—blue implies calm, cool and trust;

—green implies calm, nurturing and growth;

—purple implies rich, unique, exotic;

—red implies hot, bold, exciting, fiery and daring;

—brown implies earthy, solid, old.

○ Avoid using a mixture of vertical and horizontal format slides. **Horizontal slides** are the most common format and the shape of most screens.

○ **Use graphs, diagrams, symbols and illustrations** whenever possible in preference to word slides or tables of figures.

○ Summarise word slides in **'bullet point' format**.

○ Display **one main point per slide**.

○ Use **no more than five or six words per line**.

○ Use no more than **five to seven lines per slide**—ideally no more than 20-25 words per slide.

○ **Bold, traditional sans serif type** looks best on slides.

continued ...

○ Letter height should be sufficient so the projected image is **readable from the back row** of the largest anticipated audience.

○ Don't expose a complete list of points. **Use 'build slides' for lists of points** to prevent the audience reading ahead of you. Build slides usually leave the previous point projected, but in a subdued colour, giving you a consolidated list on the last slide in the build series.

○ You may **use your logo** in your visual presentation. This can be scanned in and adds to your presentation.

○ Insert **blank slides at the beginning and end of your presentation** (that is, solid slides that block projection light and therefore leave the screen black).

○ **Trial run all slides and equipment before your presentation.** Never use a visual aid unless you have practised with it.

○ Specify **a professional standard carousel type projector**. The Kodak SAV series is an industry standard worldwide.

○ Specify a late model slide projector (eg, a Kodak Carousel 2050 or later) which has **two bulbs** with a switch-over mechanism in case one blows. Check both bulbs work before you start.

○ Ensure the **projector is correctly lined up and focused** before giving your presentation. Position the **screen at no more than a 45 degree angle** to the audience.

○ Consider **reverse projection** (projecting from behind the screen) if this is possible as this eliminates distracting equipment in front of the audience.

Note that reverse projection is also called rear projection, but don't confuse this term with projection from the rear of the room using a long lens (that is, still forward projection).

Your **slides have to be turned around** in the carousel for reverse projection as the image is reversed.

○ **Take your own carousel with you** with the slides inside. This protects your slides, keeps them in order and ensures you have a carousel that works.

continued ...

A good tip is to seal the carousel with a strip of masking tape around the lid once you have made a final check of your presentation so your slides cannot accidentally fall out or be removed by someone. Once locked in a carousel, your slides are guaranteed to be in order, unlike overheads which can become mixed up.

○ Carefully **check the bottom metal plate of your carousel to ensure it is in the '0' position** before placing it on the projector. If it is turned around accidentally, your slides may drop out the bottom, you may start at a point other than '1', or the carousel may not fit on the projector properly.

○ Always **carry or order an extension cord and a power board or double adaptor** (you always seem to need one).

○ When delivering, **look at the audience**, not at the screen. If you have a hard copy print-out of your slides, or if you have the slide details written in the margin of your script, you will not need to look at the screen to see what is projected.

○ **Don't black-out or brown-out the room**. If you use high resolution slides and a quality screen, your slides should work in a lit room. Slide technology has come a long way. High resolution computer graphics and modern screens have changed the old view that slides require a darkened room. **Dim lights slightly** if dimming facilities are available. This will usually suffice.

○ **Avoid lights shining directly on the screen** as this will white-out your image.

○ Try to pace your slides at **one every 40 to 80 seconds**.

○ **Don't leave slides on screen when they are no longer relevant.**

○ **It is preferable not to go to a blank screen** if you are using slides. A logo or title slide may be used as a 'filler' if necessary.

At a more advanced level, consider the following points:

○ Use **two or more projectors connected with a fade/dissolve unit** which gradually merges one slide to the next giving a more professional

continued ...

presentation. This eliminates the black-out between slides and the jerkiness of abrupt slide changes that occur when one projector is used.

O Ask for **pin registered slides when using more than one projector** so that your logo, headings, etc appear at the same place on the screen with each slide and do not 'jump around'.

O **Use a long lens** so that the projector can be sited at the back of the room away from the audience.

O Ask for **an infra-red remote slide changer**. This can fit neatly in your hand or coat pocket. With it, you can change slides without returning to the lectern and without the inconvenience of a cable. It frees you from your equipment and lets you master the technology, rather than have it dictating to you.

O Use **a laser pointer** if you wish to draw audience attention to items on the screen. But note warnings about laser pointers later in this chapter.

Video

Video is one of the most widely available and widely used visual presentation media—perhaps over-used. Despite its extensive use, video usually does not match the quality of 35mm slides, overhead transparencies or 16mm movie film. This is caused by both the medium itself and the method of projection.

There are several different video media and formats in use around the world. The most common are:

O three-quarter inch U-matic magnetic tape in a large cassette;

O half-inch magnetic tape in a medium size cassette which comes in three different formats—Beta, VHS and Super VHS;

O 8mm tape in a small cassette.

Different video systems are required to play three-quarter inch U-matic tapes and half-inch Beta, VHS and Super VHS tapes. Eight millimetre video tape can be played in a VHS or Super VHS player using an adaptor.

In addition, video cassette recorders (VCRs) have to comply with VHF and UHF television standards. There are three main standards used:

O PAL (used in Australia, New Zealand, the UK, Italy, Spain, Portugal, Norway, Sweden, Denmark, Finland, Austria, the Netherlands, Switzerland, South

Africa, the People's Republic of China, Hong Kong, Singapore, Malaysia and Indonesia);

○ NTSC (used in the US, Canada, Japan, Korea, Taiwan, the Philippines and a number of South American countries); and

○ SECAM (used in France, Germany, Greece, most of the Middle East, Mauritius, a number of eastern European countries including Czechoslovakia, Hungary, Poland and Russia).

An NTSC VHS video tape will not play in a PAL VHS video cassette recorder (VCR), and vice versa. So the first rule if you are planning to use video is to know the type of video tape and then specify very clearly the equipment you need. This is particularly the case when you are travelling for presentations overseas, or using a tape from another country.

To project video, you will need a VCR of the required type (U-matic, VHS/Super VHS or Beta) linked to either:

○ one or more TV monitors; or

○ a video projector which can project video on to a large screen.

One TV monitor will be suitable only for small audiences. If you have more than 10 people in your audience, you will need either several monitors around the room requiring quite a deal of cabling and special connectors, or a video projector. Most video projectors are relatively complex to set up and tune. You are well-advised to seek the help of an audio-visual expert if you need to wire up a series of monitors or set up and use a video projector.

Apart from its sometimes questionable quality and variety of standards, another disadvantage of video is that it is a 'canned' presentation. Whereas overheads or slides support you, the presenter, video is the presentation. Most videos contain images, music and voice-over. So the audience will be fully focused on the video when you use this medium and not on you, the presenter.

Video is commonly used for part of a presentation, but rarely as the major part, and never for all of a presentation. If you leave your audience watching a video for most of the presentation, you may as well stay home.

Despite these disadvantages, video is one of the most flexible and convenient forms of visual communication. A video cassette can be easily carried in your briefcase and video equipment is available in most hotel venues, conferences and training facilities around the world.

Also, there is a wide range of subject material available on video. As well as training videos and programs that can be purchased or hired, you can tape segments from news bulletins or programs on TV. But watch copyright provisions when you do. If you plan to use a tape as part of a commercial presentation or training workshop, you may need to obtain permission from the copyright owner. This 'licence' is built in to the cost when you hire a video.

A short video or segment from a longer video can make an ideal 'refresher point' in your presentation, adding variety and a change of medium. But note the advantages and disadvantages carefully.

Advantages

O   wide availability—on a broad range of subjects;

O   highly portable;

O   VCRs and TV monitors are available in most venues around the world;

O   a wide range of subject material is available including training, corporate and motivational programs as well as theatre release movies;

O   audiences generally like to see 'movies'. A video can add an element of entertainment to your presentation.

Disadvantages

O   lower quality than high resolution overheads and slides, especially when projected on to a large screen;

O   come in a complex variety of media, formats and standards, so you need to carefully check the type of video and equipment required;

O   playing through a VCR onto a TV screen is not suitable for large audiences which will require screening on several TV monitors or projection onto a big screen;

O   video projectors are large and relatively complex to set up, usually requiring an audio-visual expert;

O   vidoes are 'canned' presentations rather than a tool supporting you, so they should only be used in short bursts.

When using a video as part of your presentation, make sure it is properly cued up. Many of the older type VCR machines roll back when you press 'Stop' and need to be cued with the counter. Newer model VCRs can be cued precisely to the point where you wish to start.

If you present to a very large audience—say, 1,000 people or more—it will be difficult for the audience at the back to see you. In such situations, video is used in another way to support presenters.

A video camera can be strategically positioned in front of you to record your presentation and project it 'live' on to a large screen. The audience at the back can watch the large video screen image of you while listening to your voice through the PA system, rather than suffer eye strain trying to see you in the flesh. Rock concerts frequently use this technology to allow fans to see a star in close-up.

Taken further, a wide screen can be used and your graphic support materials such as graphs, charts, diagrams and bullet points can be projected alongside the video image of you. The result of this coordinated video/slide/live speaker link-up is a sophisticated presentation which will hold any audience's attention.

With practice, you can even develop this technique to the extent of having your bullet points appear on screen to the left or right of your face and then, by glancing slightly while you speak, you appear to be looking at the point to which you are referring.

PC presentations

The use of computers in presentations is growing rapidly worldwide and opens up exciting opportunities for presenters.

Most offices and an increasing number of homes have PCs and recent research indicates that a high proportion of information in presentations originates from a PC. It may be budget figures in a spreadsheet, a graph in a graphics package or key recommendations or proposals in a document.

Earlier this chapter I discussed how support materials such as overhead transparencies and slides can be designed on a PC and then produced on transparencies or 35mm film for projecting on an overhead projector or in a slide projector.

In this section, this technology is discussed a little further and the next step is considered. If you or someone in your organisation produces visual aids on a PC, why not project them directly from disk, avoiding the need for overheads or slides? The technology available to you is advancing rapidly and there are major benefits in direct data projection.

First, there are significant savings in both production costs and time. The cost of imaging and mounting slides or colour overheads for a major presentation can run into many hundreds or even thousands of dollars. With direct data projection, you completely eliminate this cost. Your visuals will cost only the value of time spent in creating them on a PC. Also, because you don't need to send your visuals out to a bureau or production house for imaging and mounting as slides or overheads, you save several days in preparation of your presentation.

Second, 'live' projection of your information gives you much greater flexibility as you can change your visuals at any time right up to the start of your presentation—or even during your presentation. This can be an advantage when new information arrives or if you have a bright idea just before your presentation. If you are projecting your visuals direct from a PC, you can make these changes minutes, or even seconds, before your presentation. This does not reduce the need to prepare well in advance, but it does allow the opportunity for fine-tuning presentation visuals which is not possible with other visual aids such as slides.

Changes during a presentation can add audience interactivity and make your presentation dynamic. For instance, audience suggestions or adjustments to figures such as a budget can be keyed in and appear instantly on the screen. This can be very impressive when you are presenting plans or proposals for feedback and approval. Minor changes can be made on the spot, letting you involve your audience and work with them. 'Live' changes are certain to impress most audiences.

Two main methods of PC data projection are available:

1. liquid crystal display (LCD) panels connected to an overhead projector; or

2. data projectors which project directly from a PC or disk.

LCD panels

LCD panels sitting on top of overhead projectors came into popular use in the 1980s. In the main, this technology has been overtaken by data projectors. But there are still a large number of LCD panels in use.

In simple terms, an LCD panel is a liquid crystal display similar to a laptop computer screen that is transparent (that is, it has no backing as a laptop screen does). The LCD screen connects to the monitor port at the back of a computer and acts like a normal computer screen displaying your data or images. Because it is transparent, when you place the LCD panel on top of an overhead projector, the screen image in the panel is projected by the overhead projector.

The main limitation of LCD panels is not the panels themselves, but overhead projectors with which they are used. LCD technology has developed substantially as demonstrated by the latest laptop and notebook computers with active matrix and Thin Film Transistor (TFT) colour screens. But many of the overhead projectors in use in offices and training rooms around the world are old, poorly maintained, dirty or of too low wattage to work effectively with LCD panels.

The brightness and clarity of images projected by an LCD panel depend on the power of the projector. So, if you are going to use an LCD panel and overhead projector to project data, ensure that you use a high wattage, modern projector. Old clunkers are just not up to the task.

Also, you should use a full colour LCD panel with a 16.7 million colour palette which will project one million plus colour shades. Early models were mono (black and white only) or limited in colour capabilities.

You should note also that different cables and connectors are required for IBM type and Apple Macintosh computers. However, connectors for both types of computers usually come with LCD panels. But check your equipment fully as connectors are frequently misplaced.

As well as being able to project computer data, most modern LCD panels also support PAL, NTSC and SECAM video. This means you can connect your LCD panel and overhead projector to a VCR and project videos. However, the same quality issues arise unless you are using a high quality overhead projector.

Advantages

O   projection of data directly from a PC in 'real time' (what is on the computer monitor is what you get projected on the screen) saves the cost of producing overhead transparencies (foils) or slides and provides flexibility for last-minute changes;

O   direct projection also allows higher levels of interactivity with audiences—eg, audience suggestions can be keyed up on the screen or adjustments made to figures during a presentation;

O   LCD panels can sit on top of, and project data through, standard overhead projectors which are widely available;

O   they can project PAL, NTSC and SECAM video as well as PC data;

O   they are less costly than PC projectors.

Disadvantages

O   older model LCD panels project modest to poor quality images;

O   they are limited in image quality by overhead projectors, most of which do not have sufficient wattage to project bright images from an LCD panel. In most cases, lights have be turned off or substantially dimmed when using an LCD panel presentation which can be a major disadvantage in many circumstances;

O   three pieces of equipment are usually required—a computer, an overhead projector and an LCD panel.

Some new model LCD panels have an in-built or attached 'floppy' disk drive which allows you to project a presentation from a 3.5 inch disk, eliminating the need to have a computer connected. This reduces the amount of equipment and computer knowledge needed. However, if you drive your presentation from a disk, the panel will only read what is on the disk. Without a computer connected, you lose the capability to make changes to data or images.

LCD panels are provided by a range of companies including Kodak, Sony, 3M, In Focus Systems and Proxima.

Data projectors

A growing range of high quality, multi-purpose data projectors is becoming available which takes presentation technology to a new level. New generation data projectors are light, portable, reasonably robust, easy to use and can project high quality visuals from virtually any source or even several sources.

Most of the new generation data projectors offer 'three in one' capability. They can project data or video from:

O a computer (IBM standard or Apple Macintosh);

O a diskette in an in-built or attached 3.5 inch disk drive; or

O a VCR (PAL, NTSC and SECAM).

Single-gun data projectors, so-called because they use a single halogen lamp projecting an image from an in-built active matrix or TFT LCD screen, are increasingly replacing older style three-gun video and data projectors identifiable by their three coloured lamps.

Presenters do not need to know how these projectors work. From a presenter's point of view, their major advantage is their simplicity. Most single-gun data projectors have only two cables—one to connect to a PC and one to power. If you use the in-built disk drive, you do not even need a computer connected. A presenter can simply plug in the projector, insert a disk containing the presentation, pull the small remote control out of its holder and begin.

PC projectors are now supplied by a growing list of manufacturers including Epson, In Focus Systems (LitePro series), Sony, NEC and Proxima.

Data projectors share most of the same benefits as LCD panels, but offer additional advantages in quality, brightness of image and portability.

Advantages

O like LCD panels, PC projectors allow projection of data directly from a computer in 'real time' (what is on the computer monitor is what you get projected on the screen) which saves the cost of producing overhead transparencies (foils) or slides which can be considerable for large presentations, and provides flexibility for last-minute changes;

O direct projection also allows higher levels of interactivity with audiences— eg, audience suggestions can be keyed up on the screen or adjustments made to figures during a presentation;

O modern data projectors have high wattage bulbs which project a clear, bright image even with lights on in a venue;

O latest model data projectors are light and portable, allowing a presenter to carry a laptop computer and a projector when travelling (they will even fit in an airline overhead locker);

○ you do not need a computer to use a data projector. Many have a built-in disk drive allowing a presentation to be projected from a floppy disk;

○ they can project PAL, NTSC and SECAM video as well as PC data and most have in-built speakers for full sound capability.

Disadvantages

○ cost—like all new technology, data projectors are relatively expensive. However, prices are falling all the time and data projectors can be hired in major cities.

Presentations software

To project text, images or data from a computer or disk, this information first has to be prepared in a format suitable for projection. This requires software.

No special software is necessary to produce basic visual aids. Clear, easily readable text slides can be produced in a word processing program. Graphs, charts and tables of figures such as financial information can be produced in a spreadsheet. These are software programs that many executives already use.

However, a range of special presentation software packages has evolved and become popular in the 1990s and these offer major benefits to presenters. The key advantages offered by presentations software over other packages such as word processing and spreadsheets are that they provide:

○ pre-formatted page sizes to suit projection as overheads, 35mm slides or directly from a PC (called Screenshow);

○ a range of templates with colour backgrounds and type styles already in place. You can simply 'point and click' to choose a template that suits you, then click on a slide and start typing;

○ automatic 'build' facilities to allow you to expose one point at a time in multi-point slides;

○ a wide choice of transition effects such as dissolves, fades and wipes to move from one slide to the next, accessible at the click of a mouse button;

○ some easy drawing capabilities such as lines, arrows, shapes which can be filled with colours, star bursts, etc (these are designed to be basic and simple in presentations software and you do not have to be a graphic artist to use them);

○ special typefaces and type effects such as shadows and embossing which give a professional appearance on screen;

○ a library of clip art offering drawings, illustrations, cartoons and other special effects to add interest and impact to your presentations.

A presenter with modest computer skills and an eye for colour coordination and design can produce very attractive, semi-professional presentation visuals quickly and easily using specialist presentations software. Widely available specialist presentation software packages include:

O   Microsoft® PowerPoint®;

O   Adobe Persuasion™;

O   Lotus Freelance™;

O   Harvard Graphics™;

O   Novell Presentations™;

O   Cricket Presents™.

Most are available for both Microsoft Windows and Apple Macintosh computers.

These programs are specifically designed for executives with no specialist graphics training, typesetting knowledge or design experience. Most functions are automated or accessible through menus which simply require you to 'point and click'.

Another benefit of presentations software programs is that most provide a notes facility. Once you have made your slides, this facility allows you to enter a notes section which places each of your slides on the top half of a page with an embedded text block at the bottom for typing your notes. All you have to do is click on the text section and start typing your notes directly under the relevant slide, and then move to the next slide.

Notes pages can be printed out on a standard black and white laser printer and provide excellent speaker's notes for you to use when presenting, as you can see a print out of each slide as well as your accompanying notes.

There is also a range of more specialised graphics software which can also be used to produce presentations. Graphics software offers superior design capabilities, but requires more graphics knowledge and is slightly harder to use. Leading graphics software packages include:

O   Adobe Freehand™;

O   CorelDraw™;

O   Harvard Graphics™ and Harvard Draw™;

O   Lotus Freelance™;

O   ClarisDraw™ and ClarisImpact™.

There are also a number of utilities to help you manage and control PC presentations. These include:

○ *Infra-red mouse*
If you are using a computer with an LCD panel or data projector to present, you will be restricted in movement if you have to be near the computer to change slides with the keyboard or mouse. An infra-red mouse will allow you to roam away from your PC or stand at a lectern. Infra-red 'mice' usually have an effective range of five to 15 metres and operate in exactly the same way as a standard mouse, except commands are sent by infra-red signals from the hand-held mouse to a small receiver unit plugged into your computer.

○ *Remote viewer and control unit*
If you use a laptop or notebook computer with a small screen to drive your presentation, you may not be able to see your visuals while presenting without turning around and looking at the big screen. Remote viewer and control units such as the Videoshow Presenter™ go one better than an infra-red mouse as they provide a small control panel and screen that fits in your hand. The presenter is able to see what is being projected on the hand-held miniature screen and change slides either forwards or backwards using the control keys on the unit. Units such as the Videoshow Presenter™ even allow you to preview your next slide on the small hand-held screen before the audience sees it, and then reveal it to the audience—this is particularly useful if you lose your place or cannot remember what is on the next slide. This is a good example of how technology is helping presenters.

Another example of remote control technology to support your visual presentation is the Pro Presenter™ (available only for Apple Macintosh computers).

○ *Clip art*
In addition to clip art provided with presentations software packages, you can purchase CDs of full colour clip art to dress up your presentations and add interest. A range of industry and sector specific artwork is available as well as generic illustrations, drawings, cartoons, logos and type effects.

It is advisable to invest in some clip art if you make regular presentations as the standard clip art in popular presentations software packages such as Microsoft® PowerPoint® is widely used by presenters and audiences become over-exposed to stock illustrations. CDs of clip art with thousands of illustrations are available for $50 to $100.

As discussed earlier in this chapter, the days of sticky tape and Letraset have gone for presenters. Today, high standard presentations can be produced quickly and easily on a desktop using PCs and simple-to-use presentations software. This growing area parallels the desktop publishing revolution and is referred to as 'desktop presentation'.

Increasingly, presenters will find computer technology a faster, more efficient and more reliable way of producing their presentations.

CHECKLIST FOR USING
LCD PANELS AND DATA PROJECTORS

Equipment varies widely, but the following general guidelines should be carefully noted in using LCD panels and data projectors:

○ **Rehearse with your equipment before a presentation**. Never stand up and try to use sophisticated equipment without becoming fully familiar with it. Remember 'only poor workers blame their tools' when things go wrong.

○ If you cannot get access to equipment before the day of your presentation, turn up early and ask to **try it out before the audience arrives, or use a luncheon break to do a 'dry run'**.

○ Arrange to **have an audio-visual technician available to assist** you if possible.

○ **Double check all cables are properly connected** and working.

○ **Use an overhead projector or data projector with two bulbs** (A and B). If one blows, you can simply switch to the spare. But check that the spare works beforehand. Sometimes a previous user does not replace a bulb when it blows.

○ **Ensure you have adequate battery life** if you are using a laptop or notebook computer, or that you have it connected to a power supply.

○ **Tape all cables to the floor** to prevent people accidentally tripping over them and disconnecting your equipment.

○ If you are using a computer to drive your presentation, have it positioned discreetly out of the line of sight of the audience. **You want people looking at you and your presentation—not at your equipment**.

Multimedia presentations

The rapid integration of CD-ROM technology into personal computers has made possible the digital storage of text, graphics, sound such as voice or music, and even video on a single medium. CD-ROMs can currently hold up to 600 megabytes of information, compared with 1.44 megabytes on a 3.5 inch floppy disk. Soon CDs will hold up to seven times more with new compression and super density technologies developed by companies such as Sony, Philips, Toshiba and Matsushita.

Most PCs selling both to the business and home markets are now equipped with a CD-ROM drive and sound capabilities. This is pushing the presentation power of PCs even further.

Whereas older PCs can only store text and graphics, the CD-ROM revolution has made possible *multimedia* presentations incorporating text, graphics, sound and video which can be played by a PC. When connected to a data projector, a CD-ROM-equipped PC can project full multimedia presentations.

While only a few years ago, the most exciting development in presentations was audio-visual—the combination of sound and visuals— today multimedia is the fastest-growing segment of the presentations market. Batteries of slide projectors driven by a tape unit and video projectors the size of small refrigerators have given way to computers driving sophisticated presentations.

The production of multimedia presentations is, at this stage, a job for professionals. But this technology does illustrate the direction of presentations.

Specialist software such as Macromind Director™ are used for the production of multimedia presentations.

Video and PC conferencing

Another innovation made possible through PC technology, telecommunications and the latest projection systems is video and PC conferencing.

Once a teleconference was a telephone conference involving voice only. Today we can use video and satellite links to bring people together or to make presentations from remote locations. However, while video is readily available, satellite link-ups and transponder costs are very high and are usually used only for major international conferences or product launches.

With PCs able to be linked via modems through standard telephone lines or cable, a new method of presentation called PC conferencing is available. For instance, a plan and budget could be presented at head office to a group of executives, but managers in other cities or States may also have to be briefed. Instead of bringing the group together physically for one short presentation, the presentation could be set up on a PC at head office linked via modem to a PC in each remote office.

Then a telephone conference could be arranged with participants speaking over the phone and simultaneously seeing data on a computer screen or projected with a data projector in front of them.

Because the PC link is 'live', data can be changed and proposals thrashed out during the meeting. As the budget or points are revised, changes appear instantly on each screen, giving full interactivity and involvement.

As traditional telephone lines (called narrowband because of their limited capacity to carry data) are replaced by broadband fibre optic cables, PC conference links will be able to carry video images and sound as well as text and graphics, making possible full interactive presentations to people in remote locations.

Apple Computer has already launched a digital camera which can capture video images and transfer these directly to disk for incorporation into multimedia documents or transmission to other locations. Other PCs are also being developed with in-built video cameras that can record video images directly. This will make possible direct PC presentations where an audience will be able to hear and see you as well as your data on their screen.

While this technology will not replace human contact, it will be an important form of presentation in many situations in the future. For instance, it is costly and time inefficient for a national or international corporation to bring a group of executives from different cities or countries physically together for a one-hour presentation and discussion. Often it is difficult to 'visualise' and understand issues from a voice-only presentation via telephone. In such circumstances, a PC presentation is a way of communicating with a group or including people who cannot physically attend a presentation.

Only a brief look at cutting edge technologies is provided in this book as our primary focus is on practical everyday presentation techniques. But it is worth being aware that these technologies are coming and they further underline the need to recognise the role of computers in communication and presentations.

This chapter has given practical tips and advice on a range of visual presentation aids from the humble flip chart and whiteboard to advanced multimedia presentation technologies.

There is no excuse for business executives, trainers, academics, researchers or conference and seminar speakers who present to an audience with handwritten or typed overheads that are unreadable. There is a range of technologies available which allow you to produce visual communication aids to suit any audience, time frame and budget.

Apologies count for little. Don't get up and apologise to your audience if your visuals can't be read. This only accentuates your lack of professionalism. Take the time to prepare quality visual aids and you will dramatically increase the success of your presentations.

Other equipment and facilities

There are a number of other basic pieces of equipment and facilities which you will need to be able to use effectively as a presenter. The final section of this chapter overviews some of the other common presentation aids and provides guidelines and tips on how to use them effectively.

Checklists are again provided for the most important equipment.

Lecterns

Speeches and presentations are commonly delivered from a lectern or rostrum. A lectern provides a place for you to place your notes. Some modern lecterns also contain controls for slide changing or dimming lights. If you have extensive notes, or need to use controls that are lectern-mounted, you will need to work from a lectern.

However, a lectern is not designed or intended as a structure to lean on or hide behind. Many presenters cling to a lectern like a drowning person clutches a life raft, or retreat behind it so that only their head protruding above it is visible to the audience. Hiding behind a lectern reduces the level of contact between a presenter and the audience. Many modern presenters are moving away from lecterns, choosing to work from an overhead projector, or walking around on the floor of the room closer to the audience. This requires practice. Breaking free from the lectern also can be assisted by modern presentation aids such as infra-red control units which are discussed later in this chapter.

Microphones

You may not need a microphone for many presentations, particularly when you are presenting to small groups. However, with larger groups and in certain venues, you will need to use a microphone.

Given that many presenters have more than their share of problems with microphones which screech, whistle, pop or fade, it is useful to understand the basics of microphone technology.

Microphones are either:

O directional—they pick up sound only from a prescribed direction, usually right in front; or

O multi-directional—they pick up any sound from any direction within a reasonable distance.

The main types of microphones you are likely to encounter are:

1. *Lectern-mounted*
   These are the most common. Usually lectern 'mikes' are mounted on a flexible tube and connected by cable to a public address amplification system. Many seem to pick up every bump and rustle of papers on the lectern and amplify it through the room.

2. *Stand-mounted*

    These are usually identical to lectern-mounted microphones except they are mounted on a stand. The main difference is that you do not have a lectern to hide behind.

3. *Radio microphones*

    Cableless radio microphones are becoming increasingly popular as they free a presenter to step away from the lectern and walk around. Small radio microphones can be clipped on to your jacket (or tie for men). These are connected to a small transmitter about the size of a cigarette packet which can attach to your belt or fit inside a pocket. Usually a small antenna lead hangs from the transmitter. With a clip-on radio microphone fitted and turned on, you are 'wired for sound'.

4. *Radio microphones—hand-held*

    Another type of radio microphone is the size of a traditional hand-held microphone with a transmitter fitted inside and a short antenna lead hanging from the bottom. These are often passed around an audience during question time and less often used by presenters.

5. *Studio type boom microphones*

    In large venues, audio-visual specialists may set up boom microphones similar to those used in TV studios. These are traditional microphones mounted on booms or hung from the ceiling above you out of view of the audience.

CHECKLIST FOR USING A MICROPHONE

Most of the problems encountered with microphones are easily avoidable. Here are some tips for using a microphone:

❏ **Test the volume** of any microphone before your presentation. Test it using your normal speaking voice—not by tapping on it, blowing in it or whistling. Note the optimum distance which you should speak from it.

❏ Allow for a room full of people to absorb some sound, so **set volume slightly higher than normal if practising in an empty auditorium**.

❏ **Adjust the height** of a lectern or stand-mounted microphone to suit you before speaking. If you have to stoop, you will look like you are cringing. If you have to angle your voice up, you may appear arrogant and aloof (see 'Body language' in Chapter 9).

continued ...

O   **Don't tap the microphone** to see if it is working. Just start speaking confidently.

O   **Don't clear your throat into the microphone**. This will sound like minor explosions to the audience.

O   **Speak towards, but over a microphone**, not directly into it for best results.

O   **Don't adjust the microphone after you start talking**. This will cause loud cracking and thumping noises to be broadcast through the PA system.

O   **Avoid 'popping' your Ps or hissing your Ss**. Adjust your distance to the microphone if you hear any feedback, popping or hissing.

O   **Don't speak with your head turned away** from the microphone (eg, when looking at the screen) if you are using a directional microphone.

If you are using a radio microphone clipped to your tie or jacket:

O   **Ensure cords are tucked neatly inside your clothing**. This is not only for appearance. It will prevent you getting the cords caught and unplugging yourself.

O   **Don't clip a radio microphone where it will rub or bump against jewellery** such as a necklace or brooch. This will create noise and static.

O   **Turn your radio microphone** on before your presentation.

O   **Don't forget to turn a radio microphone off when you finish** and leave the stage. An urban myth has developed around stories of presenters who finished their presentation and went outside and bemoaned their dull and lifeless audience while their microphones were still turned on. Another story tells of a presenter who went to the bathroom while still 'wired for sound' and regaled the audience with grunts, groans and eventual sighs as he went about his business.

Screens

Screens ain't screens, to parody a popular advertising claim for oil. There are, in fact, many different types of screens available, including screens which will work quite effectively in normal lighting.

While the technical aspects of screens are largely considerations for audio-visual and staging specialists, it will help most presenters to have at least a broad understanding of what is available to know what to ask for if you have a choice.

You may have noticed that some screens are shiny white, some matte white and some are a grey or silver. Modern screens are made from a number of materials ranging from white vinyl and cloth to new 'high-tech' fibreglass and metallic covered surfaces. Screen technology has become very sophisticated.

Screens with very white surfaces are highly reflective—what is called high gain. This is achieved by coating the screen surface with metallic or fibreglass finish. High gain (highly reflective) screens are very effective for showing clear images even in a lit room. However, their viewing angle is relatively narrow—only around 60 degrees.

So high gain screens are a good choice for smaller groups seated within a 60 degree arc (that is, 30 degrees each side of the centre line) in a bright room. They are not very effective in a very wide conference situation where people at the sides may be at a sharp angle to the screen.

Low gain (less reflective) screens are matte white. These offer a viewing arc up to 100 degrees (that is, 50 degrees each side of the centre line). Low gain screens are therefore preferable for large audiences. However, they are less effective than high gain screens in bright light and may require room lights to be dimmed during presentations.

Alternatively, there are a number of new screen surfaces which are grey in colour, called silver lenticular. Their metallic surface is particularly suited to rooms which cannot be darkened or where lighting is necessary, such as when the audience has to be able to write to take notes.

SCREEN TECHNOLOGY

Type	Qualities	Use
White highly reflective (high gain)	Narrow viewing arc (60 degrees). Quality images in high ambient light	Suitable for small to medium audiences. Bright rooms. Ideal for overhead transparencies and video
White matte (low gain)	Wide viewing arc (100 degrees). Medium light qualities	Suitable for large audiences, needs dimmed lights. Slides, overhead transparencies and video
Silver (grey) lenticular	Narrow to medium arc (60–90 degrees). Quality images in medium light	Suitable for medium to high ambient light. Suit slides. Not suited for overhead transparencies or video

FIGURE 7.4 *A range of screens are available for presentations*

When reverse projection is used (with the projectors behind the screen displaying the image from the back), a special type of plastic screen material is used. This is very expensive fabric. Care should be taken in storing and transporting all screens, especially reverse projection screens.

Infra-red remote slide changers

Both slide projectors and PC presentations can be operated using an infra-red control unit. Infra-red remote control units are widely available for professional 35mm slide projectors such as the popular Kodak SAV carousel series.

A small infra-red changer can be held in your hand when giving a presentation and gives you total control over slide changes. This is a highly desirable aid as it removes your dependence on the lectern and avoids the need for cabling.

Infra-red control units are usually highly sensitive and do not need to be pointed directly at the slide projector or PC to operate. They will usually operate well when pointed within a 30 degree arc of the projector. They will even operate effectively inside the pocket of a jacket. So you do not need to make exaggerated pointing gestures with an infra-red control unit or wave your arms as if you are conducting an orchestra.

Laser pointers

Instead of a traditional wooden or metal pointer, you can opt to use a laser pointer, a small unit like a slim torch which projects a red laser beam. Laser pointers can operate up to 50 metres and, therefore, are useful for pointing out information on the screen when you are a distance away.

But laser pointers can be a mixed blessing for presenters. They work well if your hands are steady as a rock when you are presenting. However, most presenters—even experienced, confident ones—find that a laser pointer only gives a graphic demonstration to the audience that their hand is shaking. If this is the case, avoid using them.

Teleprompters

The teleprompter was developed for television comperes and news readers, but is now used extensively in major business presentations such as annual general meetings, product launches, conferences and symposia. Also known by a brand name, Autocue, the teleprompter works by reflecting a typed script from a computer terminal in one or more glass reflectors in front of the presenter.

For presentations, the glass reflectors are sited just below the presenter's eye level so that he or she can read from them, while appearing to be looking directly at the audience. The computer terminal containing the script is located off-stage and an operator scrolls the text at the required speed for the presenter to read in a natural way.

Most presenters have two or even three reflectors—with one slightly to the left and one slightly to the right, so that he or she can look left, right and centre, making contact with all sections of the audience. In many cases, audiences are unaware that a presenter is reading a script from a teleprompter.

Teleprompters are an effective alternative to reading from typed pages which results in a total loss of eye contact with an audience. However, it is critical to rehearse with a teleprompter before trying to use one to give a presentation. It is reasonably tricky to get used to reading from a scrolled script reflected in a glass panel and departing from the prepared script can cause havoc when using a teleprompter. If you venture off the script, the teleprompter operator will not know whether to slow down or speed up for you to find your place again.

A useful tip is to always take a hard copy of your presentation with you to the lectern or have a copy in your coat pocket—just in case.

Because teleprompters are still unfamiliar to many presenters, a special checklist has been compiled to use if you have to deliver a presentation from a teleprompter.

CHECKLIST FOR USING A TELEPROMPTER (AUTOCUE)

O **Deliver your script to the teleprompt operator with plenty of time.** Usually a teleprompt machine will be able to take your script from a computer disk. (If providing your speech on disk, save the document as an ASCII (text only) file with no formatting).

O **Allow rehearsal time** to have at least one, and preferably two complete run throughs with the teleprompt operator so he or she knows your speed and so you can get used to the scrolling.

O **Read your script out loud** in rehearsal exactly the way you intend to deliver it to your audience.

O **Ensure the reflector screens are adjusted at the correct height and angle** so you can see your script easily from where you stand at the lectern or when moving about.

O **Use at least two reflector screens** so you can look left and right to cover your audience.

O Don't stare at the reflector screens. **Glance away from time to time** to create a natural appearance.

O . **Advise the teleprompt operator if you plan to depart from the script.** Do so with caution.

Summary

O Find out what equipment and facilities you will need, or will be required to use.

O Make sure you are briefed on using all the relevant equipment and facilities before your presentation. Ask for advice, or call in a specialist.

O Decide which type of visual support you will use—flip charts, whiteboards (traditional or electronic), overhead transparencies, slides, video or data projection from a PC or disk. Familiarise yourself thoroughly with the type of presentation technology selected.

O Decide whether you want to:
—make your own visual support manually (eg, on a photocopier);
—make your own visual support on a PC and have it 'imaged' by a bureau;
—have your entire visual presentation prepared by an in-house specialist or production house.

O Follow the checklists provided in this chapter to help you effectively use:
—whiteboards;
—flip charts;
—electronic whiteboards;
—overheads;
—35mm slides;
—LCD panels and data projectors;
—microphones;
—teleprompters.

8

Practice and rehearsal

Every book on public speaking and presentations emphasises the importance of practising and rehearsing. Like other steps of preparing for a presentation outlined in this handbook, you should not skip over this stage. No athlete can perform without having run hundreds of races both physically and in his or her mind. No singer can reach the high notes and stay in tune without having sung every song in her or his repertoire hundreds of times before. Even though we all believe we are good drivers, no racing driver would attempt a fast lap without having driven thousands of kilometres in practice.

The common excuse by presenters is that they don't have time to practise and rehearse. In today's fast-paced age, free time certainly seems to be in short supply. And, despite all the labour-saving devices and time management systems developed by mankind, we seem to have less free time every day. Think of it another way. Do you have time to waste?

Standing up to deliver a presentation that you have not fully prepared, including practice and rehearsal, is wasting time—yours and your audience's. Without practice and rehearsal, it is highly probable that you will forget parts of your presentation, waffle in some places instead of being to the point, lose the audience's attention because you will be too busy focusing on what you are doing, and you will probably go over time.

Practice and rehearsal are critical for every presentation. You should not even think about giving a presentation that you have not presented at least three times before in live rehearsals or practice sessions by yourself.

It is important that you practise and rehearse your presentation out loud in full the way you intend to deliver it. This will help you get used to the flow of the presentation and it will allow you to estimate timing.

'Talk to the cows'

To practise and rehearse effectively, you should either work with a tolerant and constructive friend, or find a quiet place with no one around. One prominent politician from a rural electorate used to draft his speeches, and then go out and practise them on the cows in the paddock.

You may not be able to follow this advice literally, unless you live in the country. But the principle is useful. A living room or bathroom will work just as well. Only by practising your script out loud can you discover those words or phrases that cause you trouble and which may require rewriting. You must hear how your script sounds, not just how it reads. Listen to your own presentation and you will hear the parts that are working and those that sound a little flat.

Memorise your opening

A technique which will ensure you get off to a good start is to memorise your opening—the first three or four minutes of your presentation. Research studies indicate that people form an opinion about us in anywhere from 30 seconds to three minutes. Those first few minutes of a presentation are critical. In Chapter 6 it was strongly recommended that you do not try to memorise an entire presentation. But it is feasible to memorise the first few minutes. Having your opening committed to memory will allow you to start strongly and confidently which will make a positive first impression on your audience.

In addition, memorising your opening will boost your self-confidence. A nervous, shaky opening will have your audience shifting uneasily in their seats and will add to your nervousness. But, once you have started well, you will find things will go easier. You will relax a little once you get into it.

Write your own introduction

Your presentation is also affected in those first few minutes by your introduction. Usually this is done by a chairperson or MC who tells the audience a little about you before you speak.

Introductions can get your whole presentation off to a bad start unless managed carefully. Yes, that's right; manage your introduction. Don't leave it to chance.

Frequently, presenters are introduced with wrong information; or else important qualifications are not mentioned which would help the presenter establish credibility from the outset. Just as bad, or worse, are introductions which over-sell you. A glowing build-up can whip audience expectations to a such a level that anything you do is going to be an anti-climax.

It may sound egotistical, but you should write your own introduction. This is the only way to control what is said about you in the important minutes before you present. Most professional speakers have a short typewritten introduction which they send to the organisers beforehand or hand to the chairperson before their presentation. Most organisers and chairpersons will be happy for you to provide an introduction as it saves them a chore and often embarrassment.

Most importantly of all, it ensures your introduction is accurate. It is embarrassing to get up to give a presentation and begin with: 'Ladies and gentlemen, I am really the Marketing Director of Acme Corporation, not the Managing Director, and I have a degree in business—not a PhD in physics!'

Summary

O Practise and rehearse your entire presentation in full out loud at least three times before delivery.

O Memorise the first two to three minutes of your opening to make a good start.

O Write a short introduction for yourself and give this to the organisers or chairperson to ensure you are introduced appropriately—with the correct qualifications, title, and without understatement or overstatement.

9

Delivery of your presentation

The day or evening has arrived. This is it. You have come to the point of giving your presentation and the butterflies are fluttering in your stomach, your palms are a little sweaty and you may have laid awake the night before thinking about what you are going to say and do.

The key question asked by every presenter is: 'How do I control nerves?' This chapter provides useful advice and tips on reducing nervousness as well as other aspects of delivering a presentation including dress, projecting your voice and body language.

Remember though, the advice throughout this book: proper preparation is the main ingredient ensuring good delivery. So if you have skipped over previous chapters, work back through them. As Dale Carnegie advised: 'A well-prepared presentation is nine-tenths delivered' (Carnegie, 1957, p. 29).

Dress and personal presentation
Even before you arrive at your venue to give a presentation, you should carefully consider your dress and personal presentation for the important event. The credibility of your presentation, and even the attention which the audience will pay to you in the first place, are affected to a significant extent by how you look. Remember the cliche: 'You never get a second chance to make a first impression'.

In business and professional circles, well-established codes and expectations exist on dress. Power dressing was in vogue in the 1980s, but the Wall Street image has softened considerably in the 1990s. Nevertheless, according to research, a short man in glasses, wearing a beige or brown suit will have lower audience impact and credibility. A tall, grey-haired speaker in a dark blue suit with a white shirt and a bright, contrasting (but not too bright) tie will have higher credibility. Prejudice this may be, but that's what various studies show.

Presentation specialists also advise that men with facial hair have lower attention ratings with audiences than cleanly shaven men. This is probably because, from a distance, the audience is less able to see the mouth and eyes of men with beards.

Women face particular challenges, especially when presenting to mixed audiences of men and women. Generally, consultants advise that women do not have to be androgynous, but they should not wear very short skirts or low-cut blouses. These will attract audience attention, but not to the presentation.

This research does not mean men should rush out and shave off a beard which they have had for 20 years and buy a toupee, or that women giving presentations need to avoid being feminine or even sexy. But you should consider dress and personal presentation carefully. Clothes, in particular, are an important feature which can be easily improved.

Men giving presentations should wear what is considered good dress in boardrooms and executive offices. There is a timeless acceptance of:

○ dark suit (navy blue, black or charcoal grey, either plain or with a fine pin stripe);

○ white or subdued coloured stripe shirt;

○ quality silk tie (can be bright but not garish);

○ black well-polished shoes;

○ dark, unobtrusive socks;

○ plain leather belt with a simple buckle.

Red carnations or handkerchiefs in the top pocket of your coat are not necessary. Some executives look 'dressed to kill' like this. But you may appear to be too sharp or flashy—more like a car salesman than a serious executive or professional.

Bow ties and other fashion accoutrements such as braces are acceptable, but move in and out of fashion, often very quickly. Be careful with trendy fashion accessories.

Ponytails, earrings, nose rings, jeans and leather jackets are not on for business presentations. While creative people in advertising and design adopt trendy, casual clothes as their 'uniform', they are out of place in the boardroom, conference hall or formal meeting room.

There is a saying that people notice your clothes when you are badly dressed. When you are well dressed, they notice the person.

Women should be well made-up (if they wear make-up), and wear business-like, but feminine clothes such as a well-cut suit, dress or skirt and jacket. Consensus among fashion writers and advisers on executive dress for women is hard to find. However, general agreed guidelines seem to be:

○ choose solid colours for flexibility;

○ don't wear colours which are so bright that they are distracting (eg, shocking pink or bright yellow);

○ avoid very bold checks and prints;

○ avoid horizontal stripes as they can make you look fatter, particularly when photographed;

○ wear discreet quality jewellery such as a simple gold necklace or brooch, rather than tacky fake pearls or costume jewellery. Also, particularly watch necklaces if using a radio microphone as large or loose jewellery can bump a radio 'mike' causing loud interference.

Counselling is available from specialist consultants and you may consider this a worthwhile investment if you regularly give presentations to groups of people.

Many young executives find business attitudes to dress ultra-conservative and rebel against what they see as overly restrictive guidelines, or even an invasion of their privacy. But if you want to join the circus, you have to wear a costume. Wear what you like at home and when going out socially, but when giving presentations, look the part. As the song says: 'Dress for success'.

Here is an additional short, simple checklist for personal presentation.

Delivery of your presentation

CHECKLIST FOR DRESS AND PERSONAL PRESENTATION

○ **Grooming should be impeccable**—hair neatly brushed, out of your face; men should be freshly-shaven; women should have fresh make-up.

○ **Shoes should be well polished.**

○ **Never wear new shoes** to an important presentation. Hurting feet will distract you.

continued ...

○ For men, **make sure you are wearing matching socks**. It is surprising how many speakers stand on a raised stage before an audience with mismatched socks.

○ For women, **check your stockings**. Carry a spare pair in your handbag because a hole or ladder may be visible to the audience—or at least you will think it is, causing you to be self-conscious.

○ Wear discreet **jewellery**. Men and women should wear simple rather than 'loud' flashy watches and women should avoid loose necklaces that can bump a radio microphone.

○ **Avoid bulging pockets**. Take bundles of keys, loose change, packets of cigarettes and other bulky items out. Your suit will hang better and you will avoid jingling or rattling.

○ If you can, **buy a new suit for a major presentation**. You will feel like a million dollars and present better for it.

○ **Never dress down** for an audience. A common mistake of presenters is to try to dress in the style of their audience. For instance, if you are a city marketing executive going to talk to farmers, don't wear riding boots and a Crocodile Dundee hat. Your audience will expect you to look like a marketing professional. If they wanted a farmer to present to them, they would have invited a farmer.

Finally, you arrive at the point when you have to start talking. Maybe you will freeze when you get up there. Maybe you will forget what you were going to say. Perhaps the slides won't work.

These things won't happen. Not if you have followed all the steps discussed in the previous chapters. If you have researched your audience, checked out your venue, carefully prepared a structure and outline plan, written a script, produced some interesting visual aids, familiarised yourself with the relevant equipment and practised and rehearsed, you will find that you are launching into your presentation with enthusiasm. You will be anxious to get on with it—like a well-trained racehorse which champs at the bit when the starter's orders go out.

The following advice and suggestions, based on the experience of many veteran presenters, will further assist you in delivering a successful presentation.

Voice

No one likes the sound of his or her own voice. This is not just a human idiosyncrasy. It is because of the way we hear ourselves. We hear others through our ears, which are sophisticated audio receivers. But we hear our own voice largely through our jawbone and resonance in our head. This partly distorts the sound. We don't hear ourselves the way others hear us.

The reason most people are surprised the first time they hear their voice recorded on tape is that, notwithstanding some change that occurs in recording and playback, they are hearing themselves as others hear them for the first time.

There are several aspects of voice which you should consider.

Pitch

Your voice can be high or low in a musical sense. The vocal range of most people is around two octaves (eight notes to an octave). But presenters should normally speak around the middle of this range. There is a school of thought which holds that low voices (baritone in men and contralto in women) are more attractive to audiences and considered more influential and powerful.

You cannot fundamentally change the pitch of your voice. But you can move your pitch marginally higher or lower with practice. Try to start out a presentation with a low pitch because we all move the pitch of our voice up as we become enthused. If you start high, you will be shrieking by the end.

Inflection

Raising your voice in a tonal sense, such as going up at the end of a sentence to indicate a question, is inflection. This 'bending' of your voice, created through voluntary or involuntary muscular tension, adds meaning and emphasis.

You should try to introduce inflection into your voice for presentations. The place to try various approaches is during rehearsals. Have a friend listen and give you a critique.

Volume

Volume is the decibel level of your voice and can be increased or decreased by pushing more or less air over the vocal chords. Most people speak at a relatively constant volume, but volume can and should be raised and lowered in presentations to add variety.

You should never speak at one pitch, without inflection and with a constant volume. This is monotone speech. A monotone delivery will soon bore your audience and put people to sleep.

The raising and lowering of pitch and volume is called modulation. Modulation is important to an effective presentation. A good speaker is said to have a well-modulated voice. This generally means that good speakers intelligently vary their volume, pitch and use inflection in their voices to create variety as well as a pleasant euphony.

Clarity

Clear pronunciation and proper expression of sounds are vital for an audience to be able to understand what you are saying without difficulty. Research shows that if people have difficulty in hearing what you are saying, they will quickly 'switch off'.

Practise your voice by reading slowly and exaggerating vowel and consonant sounds. Open your mouth wide when practising. Remember the speech lessons you had at school that seemed silly at the time: 'The rain in Spain falls mainly on the plain' and 'Mrs Brown went to town...' and so on. They are good disciplines to clear up our speech which becomes lazy in everyday use.

Speed

Most of us speak too quickly. Everyday speech creates habits of babbling and excitedly speaking in broken and incomplete sentences. Presenters need consciously to slow down their delivery. It should not be too slow, as this too will create boredom. A good approach is to speak very slowly in practice. Then, with the enthusiasm and nervous energy that will come when you stand up to present, you will achieve an ideal speed.

On average, you should speak around 150 words per minute. Less than 125 words per minute is too slow and more than 175 is too fast (McMahon, 1986, p. 92). Time yourself during rehearsals and adjust your speed as well as other aspects of your voice.

Your voice can be a powerful tool if used well. Consider the enormous salaries paid to radio announcers who have voices which listeners find attractive. Even if you cannot woo and seduce your audience the way radio announcers do, you should add variation and modulation into your voice to create interest and euphony which will help your audience listen to you and make your presentation a success.

Body language

While having its roots in pop psychology rather than science, body language is now recognised as an important part of all communication and is particularly relevant in giving presentations.

Body language is 'the outward reflection of inner emotions' according to Allan Pease who wrote the best-selling book, *Body Language* (Pease, 1981). People transmit and receive non-verbal signals in every facet of their lives, from dating to standing on a stage addressing an audience.

For instance, a presenter telling an audience that a new product is the most exciting development in the company's history will not be convincing if he or she is speaking in a monotone voice standing motionless behind a lectern. By comparison, voice inflection, gestures like an outstretched hands or pointing a finger at the sky, animated facial expressions and movement communicate excitement and involvement and tell us through body language that something is important.

In our personal lives, if we are telling someone a story and they are constantly looking away and fiddling, their body language tells us they are not really interested even if they say they are. Consider also how body language can make words mean the opposite of their normal meaning, such as someone saying 'You're an idiot' to a colleague. If the words were said with a serious expression, the person would most likely take offence. But, if the speaker was smiling and stretched an arm around the shoulders of the person being addressed, the message is clearly a friendly jibe.

Importantly for presenters, body language is a two-way street. Not only does a presenter communicate with his or her audience through body language, but an audience sends signals to a presenter through body language. A presenter can gain valuable feedback from an audience by reading body language.

The key elements of body language for presenters can be summarised in an acronym that is easy to remember—SOFTEN—where each letter of the word represents the first letter of six key techniques.

Smile

There is no more powerful communication among humans than a smile. A smile can solve arguments, soothe hurt feelings, begin relationships, reassure friends and convey appreciation. In presentations, it is not appropriate for you to be grinning like a Cheshire cat, but a light smile makes you appear more friendly and human and helps build rapport with an audience.

Smile at appropriate opportunities when you are presenting. And look for audience smiles in return. If people smile back, it is a sign that they are listening and enjoying your presentation.

Open stance

Folded arms across the chest is a classic closed stance. This conveys resistance, lack of acceptance and even belligerence. Other examples of a closed stance are hunched shoulders with hands together, legs crossed and head down looking at the floor. By comparison, an open stance is characterised by outstretched arms or hands, looking up, chest out rather than hunched and feet slightly apart. An open stance conveys welcoming, trust and acceptance.

When you present, you should adopt an open stance. Likewise, watch your audience to see whether individuals are sitting with an open or closed stance. This will help you determine whether you are getting through and whether the audience is accepting what you are presenting.

Forward lean

Whether a person leans slightly forward or back also sends body language messages. Leaning back such as slumping back in a chair conveys disinterest, especially if the arms are folded across the chest as well. Standing with an steeply arched back and rocking back on one's heels conveys aloofness and is often referred to as 'looking down your nose'.

Conversely, a slight forward lean indicates interest. An interested audience will lean slightly forward in their chairs, so look for this signal. Likewise, when you are presenting, you should lean slightly forward. Try putting one foot slightly in front of the other and combine forward lean with an open stance such as stretching out your hands towards the audience. You will find this sends clear body language messages to your audience. The audience will feel you 'reaching out' to them and they will see you as receptive of them and their ideas.

Tone

Tone relates primarily to voice, but can also be expressed in other elements of body language such as gestures. A loud, thundering voice communicates power and conviction. But it can also convey aggression or pomposity. You should carefully adjust the tone of your voice to suit your topic and the audience. Vary your tone, adding light and shade. Sometimes an important point can be made by speaking momentarily in a very soft voice, causing the audience to concentrate and listen closely. On other occasions, your subject will warrant raising your voice to the heavens.

Use gestures that are appropriate such as outstretched hands which are welcoming, or raising a finger to indicate an important point. But avoid waving your arms too much and do not point your finger directly at people. In some countries this is considered very rude and offensive. Strong gestures such as punching the air with your fist may be appropriate in certain circumstances, but also sets an aggressive tone and should be used selectively.

Try to use gestures that come naturally. You should not stand rigid and motionless. Nor should you appear like a puppet on a string, making unnatural, false, exaggerated or jerky gestures. Vary your gestures. Some presenters unconsciously make the same gesture over and over. Once the novelty wears off, the audience will start noticing your favourite gesture and by the end of your presentation will be counting or laying bets on how many times you do it. The best way to identify any pet gestures you have is to rehearse in front of a mirror. This way you will see as well as hear yourself, and you can adjust any repetitive or distracting elements of your body language.

Eye contact

This is the most important element of body language in virtually any situation. Human beings around the world like others to look them in the eye when they are communicating. Forget whatever you have been told about looking over the audience's heads at the back of the room as a way of fooling people that you are looking at them. Even from 20 or 30 metres, most people can tell if you are looking them in the eye.

Clearly, you cannot make eye contact with everyone in larger audiences. But you should make direct eye contact with selected people at various points around the room.

There are two important rules on eye contact. First, vary the focus of your eye contact covering both left and right, front and rear of your audience. Avoid picking out a single spot or a particular person such as a friend or someone who is obviously interested. While this is tempting or easy to fall into through habit, others in your audience will feel left out and alienated if you play favourites. Second, never maintain eye contact too long. A few seconds is enough to say 'Hello, I am speaking to you personally'. If you look at someone too long, that person will feel self-conscious and look away. But a short glance builds rapport with your audience and creates a link.

Also, look for audience eye contact with you as a feedback medium. If you look around the room and see most people looking down, out the window or staring blankly into space, you clearly have some work to do. It's time for a refresher point such as a new visual, a story or joke or some form of audience participation to regain attention. On the other hand, when you look around a room and receive regular eye contact from people in the audience, sometimes with even the hint of a smile, it is a very reassuring feeling and a sure sign that you are in the process of delivering a successful presentation.

Nod

Another powerful element of body language is the simple silent nod. Often, a nod will accompany eye contact. When you look at someone in an audience for a few seconds while you are speaking, most people will instinctively nod, signalling they are listening to you and possibly that they agree with you. A nod indicates you have made contact—you are getting through.

Look around your audience as often as you can, make eye contact with individuals at various points and watch for nods. They are welcome signals for most presenters. You can also use a nod as part of your body language to acknowledge people during audience participation or question time.

Christina Stuart who runs Speakeasy training programs in the UK says: 'If you don't pay attention to your audience, they will not pay attention to you.'

Remember the emphasis placed on presentations as communication in Chapter 1, with communication being defined as a two-way process of building understanding. During a presentation, you usually do not have the benefit of verbal audience feedback as comments and questions are normally held till the end. The main and often the only medium for an audience to tell you what they are thinking and how they feel during a presentation is body language. As well as polishing your own body language to make it complement verbal and visual language used in your presentations, you can harvest information from audience body language and use it to make your presentations successful.

Controlling nervousness

Nervousness manifests itself in two ways when delivering presentations. First, there is that awful, fluttery feeling in the pit of the stomach which we refer to as 'butterflies'. The effects of nervousness can be debilitating, reducing our powers of concentration, seemingly blotting out our memory, leaving us short of breath and even affecting us physically such as causing our hands to shake and our knees to knock.

You are not alone in feeling nervous. Famous speakers too have felt their share of nervousness. Ed McMahon, America's Toastmaster General for many years and noted television presenter, described the feeling just before a presentation in graphic terms: 'A pervasive, infectious fear hangs in the air like diesel fumes' (McMahon, 1986, p. 3).

British politician, Lloyd George said: 'The first time I attempted to make a public talk, I tell you I was in a state of misery. It is no figure of speech, but literally true, that my tongue clove to the roof of my mouth and, at first, I could hardly get out a word' (Carnegie, 1957, p. 16).

Famous orator and British Prime minister, Benjamin Disraeli claimed that he would rather face a cavalry charge than the House of Commons for the first time. The opening speech of this noted orator was a ghastly failure (Carnegie, 1957, p. 17).

Two thousand years ago, the immortal Roman orator, Cicero, said that all public speaking of real merit was characterised by nervousness (Carnegie, 1957, p. 17).

To manage nervousness, it helps to understand that the feelings are themselves symptoms. When we face situations that cause us fear or anxiety, several physical changes occur in the body. Sensing a need for more oxygen, the heart starts beating faster, pumping more blood to key organs including the brain. This oxygen overload accounts for the feeling of light-headedness that can occur before giving a presentation and the extra blood in our limbs can cause slight shaking. Faced by fear, our brain also may trigger the release of the powerful, naturally-occurring drug in our body, adrenalin. This gives us a further 'rush'. These are normal phenomena. It is the body's way of preparing for exertion.

All in all, these are positive, performance-enhancing changes in our body. It is important to recognise that none of us can perform well without a quickening of the heart and a surge of oxygen and adrenalin. Nervousness only becomes a problem when, faced by the first strange feelings of invigoration, we start to panic, setting off a chain reaction which further speeds up the heart, causing it to pump yet more oxygen-rich blood to the brain and release more adrenalin which, in turn, causes an overdose of oxygen and adrenalin.

Nervousness can be reduced by using the following techniques:

○ *Regulating your breathing*
The first important technique to reduce feelings of nervousness is to slow down your heartbeat by regulating your breathing. Slow, deep-breathing exercises are one important way to manage the symptoms of nervousness. Don't expect instant results after three or four deep breaths. Carefully regulate your breathing whenever you feel nervous and particularly in the hour immediately before a presentation. By avoiding hyperventilation and reducing oxygen and adrenalin overload, your memory will begin to function normally again and the severe discomfort of nervousness will subside considerably.

○ *Laughter*
Another highly effective method of relaxing yourself and your audience is laughter. If possible, plan a humorous story or joke early in your presentation. Laughter causes the brain to release a chemical called endorphin which is a tranquilliser or relaxer. It has been physiologically proven that everyone feels better after a good laugh.

○ *Relaxation techniques*
Many devotees of eastern philosophies also vouch for the calming effects of practices such as yoga and various Zen mental relaxation techniques. If these work for you, use them before presentations. It really is a case of 'mind over body'. Your body is only reacting to what you are thinking.

○ *Visualisation*
You can also reduce nervousness by changing what you are thinking through visualisation. This is the technique of seeing yourself performing well and giving a successful presentation in your mind. Visualisation instils positive images in place of the negative ones which we tend to conjure up. Instead of thinking 'I'm going to be a disaster', think 'I know my subject. I'm well organised. I'm going to wow them.' It is amazing what a little self-indoctrination can do.

○ *Treating the cause rather than symptoms*
The most important step that you can take to reduce nervousness is to reduce the cause of fear which sets the body into overdrive before a presentation. Fear of giving presentations—which research quoted in Chapter 1 showed to be our most common fear—is not a fear of people. It is usually a fear of the unknown.

Presenters who do not prepare well should feel fear. They are walking into a venue which is a totally unfamiliar environment; talking to a group that they know very little about; using equipment that they have never used before; and giving a presentation that they have not practised or rehearsed. Fear in such circumstances is quite normal. The chances of failure in entering unknown territory are high.

But a presenter who has carried out detailed preparation as outlined in the eight steps presented in this book, will be facing a structured, known environment. He or she will be quite familiar with the audience; they will have checked out the venue previously; tested the equipment; structured their presentation in a logical order so that it is easy to remember; supported it with visual aids that provide a back-up for the audience as well as themselves if they happen to lose their train of thought; and they have practised several times. They will have spare bulbs in the projector; large typed notes or cue cards that they can read; and a few good stories, anecdotes or jokes up their sleeves which they can use if the audience does not seem to be warming or paying attention.

Armed with such an arsenal, a presenter is prepared to face anything. There are not likely to be any surprises. The chances of failure become remote, so the fear of giving a presentation subsides considerably.

O *Massage*
Other presenters treat themselves to a relaxing massage, such as the shiatsu technique, before a presentation. If it works for you, use it.

O *Food and drink*
It is wise to avoid drinking carbonated drinks or dairy products as these tend to dry your mouth. You should also avoid ice water as this constricts the throat which will reduce the timbre of your voice. Too much coffee or tea can also dry the throat and caffeine may make you jumpy and add rather than reduce tension.

You should eat lightly before presentations, but maintain your intake of fluids. The ideal drink before presentations is water at room temperature with lemon. Lukewarm water is gentle on your throat and lemon reduces the build-up of mucus which causes presenters to regularly clear their throat.

You should never consider using alcohol or other drugs to relax yourself before a presentation. Drugs may relax you, but they also slow down brain functions in all areas. You only need to closely watch someone who has been drinking or taking drugs to see that is not the way to deliver successful presentations.

You can effectively manage nervousness in a number of ways, but the best way is to start from the beginning with sound preparation which will put you in good shape when you come to deliver your presentation.

You will still feel a touch of 'butterflies' and your hands are still likely to shake a little before you start. This is natural in the state of 'heightened awareness' that the body achieves in preparing itself for any major activity. You cannot and should not want to eradicate the butterflies. But, with the techniques outlined, you will be able to get them flying in formation.

Nervous habits are the second manifestation of nervousness. By definition, nervous habits are involuntary or uncontrolled body language that can be distracting to an audience. Everyone has nervous habits. So don't feel bad if you or your friends have noticed you have some. In fact, to be a successful presenter, you should consciously look to identify your nervous habits. Ask your friends or objective observers to watch you closely when you are presenting, or in a pressure situation, and identify traits that regularly show up.

Nervous habits typically include:

○ fiddling with something such as playing with rings, cuff links, buttons, a necklace or your nails, or toying with a pen or the pointer;

○ moving your hands constantly—like putting them in and out of your pockets. You need to find a natural place for your hands and leave them there;

○ constantly putting on and taking off glasses;

○ clutching the lectern or back of a chair like a life raft;

○ constantly pulling an ear, eyebrows or your nose;

○ pushing or flicking back your hair;

○ scratching;

○ shuffling your feet and transferring your weight from one foot to the other;

○ rocking or swaying from side to side (this is particularly annoying as it can move you away from the microphone resulting in your voice fading in and out);

○ pacing up and down like a caged animal;

○ using set phrases or statements over and over such as 'Let me just say...' or 'Okay'.

The list goes on and on. The key point is that *you* have nervous habits. You need to discover them and bring them under control. Your body language should say 'I'm relaxed, confident and happy to be here', even if you are still feeling a little nervous inside.

Using an assistant

If you are using overhead transparencies, a video or other equipment, it may help you to have an assistant carry out some tasks. For instance, changing overhead transparencies interrupts the flow of a presenter. If your hand is a little shaky, it can be quite easy to drop transparencies on the floor or put them on at an angle.

If you use an assistant, it is even more critical that you practise and rehearse together. Having to stop and give instructions to an assistant will be more disruptive than changing overheads or loading a video yourself.

An assistant can be helpful also in last minute arrangements or errands such as getting you a glass of water, checking the volume of your microphone at the back of the room, or finding the audio-visual technician if needed. In the final moments before delivery of a presentation, you should be free to relax, concentrate and psych up for the successful presentation that is to come.

CHECKLIST FOR DELIVERING A PRESENTATION

○ **Watch for cables and wires when you walk up to speak.** You don't want to trip and fall on your face. Ask for any loose cables to be taped to the floor with masking tape.

○ **Make eye contact** with people around your audience. Look people in the eye, but don't stare too long as you will make them feel singled out and uncomfortable.

○ **Vary the pitch and inflection of your voice** when you speak, raising it to indicate questions, lowering it to conclude and round off a main point (called modulation).

○ **Vary the speed** at which you speak for effect and contrast (eg, rapid fire through a list of achievements quickly, then deliver a key objective slowly and deliberately).

○ **Vary volume.** You don't always have to speak loudly to hold attention. Try lowering your voice—even down to a hushed tone at times which will have the audience straining at the edge of their seats to hear you. This is an effective device for holding or winning back attention. But don't overdo it.

○ Don't be afraid to **use silence** for effect. A few seconds pause after a key point will let it sink in. You will also find that silence will bring audience attention back to you. Heads will look up.

○ Don't forget to **smile** occasionally.

continued ...

○ Put **genuine energy and enthusiasm** into your presentation. The audience will be persuaded to believe your message only if you look and sound like you really believe it. Get worked up, as long as you don't rant or gush.

○ Contrast seriousness with **humour**. If you have just delivered a very 'heavy' message, lighten the tone by moving to a short anecdote, telling a story or using a visual, such as a cartoon, for effect.

○ **Have an assistant change overheads** if possible so that your presentation rhythm is not constantly interrupted.

○ **Don't read your visuals off the screen**. The audience can read them quite well without you. You should focus on amplifying and adding to the key words, facts or illustrations that are on the screen. Spell out key points and give examples.

○ **Don't point with your finger on an overhead projector**. This creates a large black image of your hand projected on to the screen. Use a fine pointer or pen on the overhead projector top, with your hand away from the lit area.

○ **Don't point at information on the screen** unless you have a long pointer. Using your hand requires you to walk into the screen area, blotting out information.

○ **Don't walk in front of the projector** as a large shadow will be projected on the screen, distracting the audience.

○ **Keep to time.**

○ **Allow time at the end of your presentation to summarise** (Tell 'em what you've just told 'em) and take questions.

Team presentations

Most of this book has been about individual presentations, although the principles apply equally to situations where two or more presenters work together.

Team presentations are used very effectively by advertising and public relations agencies where presenters want to show the team of talent which will handle the account and the client wants to see more than one front person.

If you believe you can better achieve the objective of your presentation by using more than one presenter, there is no reason why you should not use a team presentation. The variety will immediately add an interest factor for the audience.

However, there are some things to watch. When you do team presentations, follow all the general rules of presentations. In addition, pay special attention to the following checklist.

CHECKLIST FOR TEAM PRESENTATIONS

○ More than one presenter adds variety and will help hold audience attention. But **keep your presentation to no more than two or three presenters** as any more will cause confusion and break the flow of your presentation.

○ **Rehearsal is critical for team presentations**. People who know their subject area are not automatically good team presenters. Practise together before giving a team presentation.

○ Each presenter must **know change points and 'throw lines'** (links) to ensure smoothness.

○ **Avoid delays** between presenters.

○ Have each team member **stay within allocated time limits**. Over-runs will cause later presenters to rush and weaken the presentation.

○ Have each team member **stay within allocated subject areas**. Encroachment into other areas will lead to duplication or hasty, impromptu editing by later presenters—sometimes with disastrous results.

○ Have a **single, standardised set of visuals**. Don't allow team members to prepare their own visuals independently as this will lead to inconsistent quality and lack of coordination.

○ Endeavour to **have a mix of men and women** in your team if possible— but don't indulge in tokenism.

○ Have a smooth **procedure for handling questions**. One effective approach is using a moderator to choreograph the presentation and direct questions to the most relevant team member. Avoid having two or more team members answer the same question if possible, as this slows down proceedings and overwhelms the questioner.

Adding 'pith, punch and polish'

As you become more experienced at delivering presentations, there are a number of advanced techniques for adding extra pith, punch and polish that will make your presentations truly memorable and add to your success.

Enthusiasm

The first tip for adding extra energy and life to your presentations is to exude enthusiasm. US poet and essayist, Ralph Waldo Emerson said: 'Nothing great was ever achieved without enthusiasm' (Bloomsbury, 1989, p. 46). An audience is more likely to believe what you say and support your proposals or recommendations if you project genuine energy and enthusiasm.

Better still, you should be passionate about your topic. Passion leads to excellence. Author Robert L. Montgomery said: 'There is just one cure for all the negative speech habits, faults and affected mannerisms—get truly excited on the right subject and 99% of the faults of your speaking will disappear' (Macnamara & Venton, 1990, p. 19).

Quotable quotes

As mentioned in Chapter 5, quotable quotes make your key points more memorable. These may be quotes that you borrow from other people such as has been done liberally in this book.

For instance, people all over the world remember famous quotes such as John F. Kennedy's call to Americans: 'Some people see things as they are and say "Why?" I dream things that never were, and say "Why not?"'

You can collect interesting and useful quotations to suit various occasions as part of your research. Make use of references such as *The Columbia Dictionary of Quotations*, or *The Oxford Dictionary of Quotations*, available in book or CD-ROM format.

The 'rule of three'

Public speaking and presentations are made easier on the ear when they have euphony—that is a pleasant sound and balance. Too many long sentences become boring and difficult to say. Too many short sentences sound staccato and abrupt.

One of the commonly used structures in public speaking is the 'rule of three' which involves the balancing of three complementary or related points. For instance, 'Veni, vidi, vici' (I came, I saw, I conquered) is an example of the 'rule of three'.

Abraham Lincoln's famous Gettysburg Address contained this sentence: 'But in a larger sense we cannot dedicate, we cannot consecrate, we cannot hallow this ground.'

George Wallace in his inaugural speech as Governor of Alabama in January 1963 said: 'I say segregation now, segregation tomorrow and segregation forever!' Whatever you think of Wallace's views, he made his point clearly (Oxford Dictionary of Quotations, 1992).

Margaret Thatcher's reported attack on communism was made all the more memorable and quotable by her use of the 'rule of three': 'Soviet Marxism is ideologically, politically and morally bankrupt'.

Ronald Reagan reportedly said of peace: 'We will negotiate for it, sacrifice for it, but we will not surrender for it'.

'Contrastive pair'

As well as matching three complementary points, orators use a contrastive pair to make a point. A noteworthy example was the conclusion of John F. Kennedy's stirring inaugural address: 'Ask not what your country can do for you; ask what you can do for your country.'

Addressing a Democratic National Convention in San Francisco, Jesse Jackson made memorable use of contrastive pairs: 'There is a proper season for everything. There is a time to sow and a time to reap. There is a time to compete and a time to cooperate' (McMahon, 1986, p. 79).

Repetition

Don't be afraid of repetition to make your point. Good speakers regularly repeat their messages—sometimes over and over. For instance, consider Winston Churchill's famous speech to Britons in the darkest hours of World War II: 'Never give in. Never give in. Never, never, never, never—in nothing, great or small, large or petty—never give in except to convictions of honour and good sense' (McMahon, 1986, p. 79).

Sincerity

In striving for special effects and impact in your presentations, avoid making your presentation sound false or contrived. It must be you. Sincerity is worth a hundred points of technique. Renowned poet Samuel Taylor Coleridge said: 'What comes from the heart, goes to the heart' (Bloomsbury, 1989, p. 133).

Remember this in giving presentations, especially when you are struggling with trying to remember your content or combating nervousness. The audience did not come for technique. They came to hear you. Speak from the heart. Remember Robert L. Montgomery's admonition that, if you get truly excited on the right subject, 99% of the faults of your speaking will disappear. Even if they don't disappear, your audience will not notice if you are presenting something you believe in with passion, enthusiasm and sincerity.

Summary

○ Dress for success in presentations. A high standard of personal grooming and executive dress is essential. Take a course or counselling in dress and grooming if necessary.

○ Men should follow the standard business 'uniform' of:

—dark suit (navy blue, black or charcoal grey, plain or with a fine pin stripe);

—white shirt or subdued coloured stripe;

—silk tie (can be bright and contrasting, but not garish);

—well-polished black shoes;
—plain leather belt with a plain buckle;
—preferably clean-shaven.

O Women should dress professionally, but be feminine:

—suit, dress or skirt, blouse and jacket;
—plain fabrics in dark colours (black, navy blue, dark grey, medium grey, maroon);
—check stockings (carry a spare pair);
—careful attention to grooming (neat hair, well-done make-up but not too much etc);
—minimum exposed skin.

O Understand your voice. Learn to modulate by varying pitch and inflection. Also, practise varying volume and speed.

O Most important of all as far as voice is concerned, speak moderately slowly and clearly. Practise speech if you need to, or undertake training.

O Pay attention to body language. Follow the SOFTEN formula to make your gestures, stance and movements complement your verbal presentation. Also, watch your audience's body language as it gives you valuable feedback on what your audience is thinking and feeling.

O Identify your nervous habits and learn to control them.

O Use the checklist provided for delivering a successful presentation.

10

After the presentation— icing on the cake

'Ladies and gentlemen, I hope you have found my presentation stimulating. Thank you for your attention.'

With that, you sit down. A huge feeling of relief sweeps over you. But wait a minute. Your presentation is not over yet. Most audiences will want to ask questions. And there are some other things you can and should do to ensure your presentation is a success.

Handouts

The first of these is leaving your audience with something to help them retain your messages. Commonly referred to as handouts, these leave-behinds can be:

O   a full printed transcript of your presentation;

O   hard copy of your visuals;

O   typed up notes of your presentation.

It is a good rule never to distribute handouts before or during your presentation. People will read your script or notes while you are presenting. Inevitably, they will be either behind or ahead of you, so they will not be listening to what you say.

The only handouts which should be distributed before a presentation are notes which may be required for the audience to participate in some exercise you are going to undertake during the presentation. But you should always try to distribute handouts of your information afterwards so your audience can re-read and retain your presentation for future reference. Handouts are, therefore, another form of aid to making your presentation a success.

The notes capability of specialist presentation software packages discussed under 'Presentation aids' in Chapter 7 provide excellent and quickly produced handouts, as they provide the audience with a hard copy of both your visuals and accompanying notes.

Answering questions

Every audience has at least one. He or she is a closet egomaniac who will find the curliest, most cutting or cutest question to throw at you.

These personality types usually spend the whole presentation thinking up their question. So don't be surprised if they ask you about something you have already covered during your presentation. They may even arrive with the question they plan to ask already in their minds, irrespective of what you say. Also, don't be surprised if there is no question—just a statement. Many 'questioners' are frustrated orators who want to hear the sound of their own voices and air their own views at any opportunity.

Don't be rude to questioners—no matter how irritating they are. The main thing to remember is that you are not really talking to them. Talk to your whole audience. If someone is rude to you, you will probably win audience sympathy and support if you keep your cool.

We would all like to be capable of the witty and cutting retorts of the great masters such as Winston Churchill who, when a woman heckler shouted, 'I wouldn't vote for you if you were the Archangel Gabriel', allegedly replied: 'Madam, if I were the Archangel Gabriel, you wouldn't be in my electorate'.

All of us have fantasised at one time or another about cutting someone down to size. But the best policy is to avoid sarcasm and putting questioners or hecklers down. Unless you have the verbal dexterity and debating skills of a Churchill, you will only find yourself in a shouting match which will have few, if any, winners.

A key step in handling questions is to establish a clear policy on questions from the outset. In consultation with the chairperson if necessary, let the audience know whether you will:

1. take questions at any time during your presentation (usually not recommended except in the most informal discussion group presentations); or

2. take questions in a formal question time at the end of your presentation. If so, set aside adequate time for this. Nothing frustrates an audience more than waiting with a question for 30 minutes and then not having the chance to ask it.

There are many types of questions. You should be aware of the following types and the best way to respond to each.

The concealed objection

These questions usually begin with give-away phrases such as 'But won't your proposal cause...' You should not be defensive. Concealed objection questions should be handled largely in the same way as an objection which involves restating or reiterating your key statements and explaining the benefits of your proposal.

The test question

This is often asked by the 'smart alec' who wants to probe your knowledge and expertise. He or she will ask questions like: 'What is the stress factor of this new alloy when applied under heat, say, to 150 degrees?' or 'Could you give us the breakdown of this budget across the five divisions and explain what difference there will be to current operations in each?'

The golden rule in handling test questions is not to try to bluff. Also, don't apologise for your ignorance. If you don't know, state this quite clearly, but offer to get the information and supply it to the questioner. Keep your promise.

The display question

This is asked by the show-off who does not really want to ask you a question. He or she wants to tell the audience how much he or she knows about the subject. Nothing pleases this type of questioner more than public recognition. So if there is no real question—and provided the statement is correct—tell this person how clever they are and move on. 'Yes, that's quite correct. Thank you for the comment.'

The challenge question

This type of question arises when someone in the audience feels that you have encroached into their area of expertise or responsibility. It is usually more a territorial dispute than a question. If this occurs, it is usually wise to retreat or correct any impression that you are coming in over someone. For instance, if a product manager issues a challenge question about your knowledge of marketing in relation to his product, you might have to explain: 'I should point out that I was speaking about the market overall, not the specific market for widgets in which you have much more knowledge than I do. I'm sorry for the confusion.'

The defensive question

Defensive questions are asked by people who may be affected by what you are proposing. They are another form of objection. You may get asked: 'But centralised ordering is part of my job and it has proven to be the only system that works. How can you prove your new system will work?'

This is a tough one. You usually have to be prepared for spirited defence if you are attacking some entrenched system or proposing a new way of doing things. Stick to your guns. Often, turning questions back on a defensive questioner will help. For instance: 'Do you feel that the current system is foolproof and without fault?'

Off the record questions

Don't be fooled into answering a question in a public place with a statement that is off the record. If you answer a question in public, it is on the record.

Yes or no questions

A questioner who asks for a simple 'Yes' or 'No' response is often aggressive and trying to manipulate you. You don't have to accept this approach. Answering questions with a carefully thought out stand-alone statement is the best policy.

'No win' questions

In a business situation, you could be asked: 'Are our falling sales due to poor management or poor selling?' If you are in management, you face the choice of either blaming yourself, or blaming the sales representatives in the audience.

Again, the carefully thought out stand-alone statement works best. You might answer: 'There are several reasons for the fall in sales. First,...' Explain the situation in a fair and balanced way.

As you listen to a question you should be deciding in your mind whether to:

O   answer it;

O   agree with it and treat it as a statement;

O   refer it to someone else such as an expert colleague;

O   defer it by asking the questioner to discuss it with you privately afterwards (effective for dealing with questions which are irrelevant to the subject under discussion or so technical that the answer would mean nothing to the audience);

- admit you don't know the answer and ask to be able to come back to the questioner with a researched response;

- throw it back to the audience. This is an effective technique if you are asked a particularly nasty challenge or defensive question. You can ask: 'Do other members of the audience feel the same way?' If you get a negative response, you are free to move on to the next question and perhaps offer to take up a discussion with the questioner privately.

A key point in answering questions is to quell immediately any emotional response or reaction you feel. Never show anger, belligerence or nervousness in answering questions.

Look upon questions positively. They are a chance to gauge audience reaction to your presentation. Enthusiastic questioning usually means you have stimulated the audience. Lack of questions is a sign that you either answered all the audience's questions in your presentation, or they are too bored to ask questions. Often, unfortunately, it is the latter.

Put a pleasant, cooperative tone in your voice when answering questions. But you don't have to grovel. Phrases such as 'I'm glad you asked me that' and 'That is a very good question' are over-used.

How to stop ramblers

A final word is warranted on how to stop those dreaded questioners who go on and on, giving a speech, without asking a question. Here are a few tips:

- look at your watch. Tap your finger on it as a signal to the questioner if necessary;

- use body language, eg, hold up your hands to indicate 'enough's enough';

- appeal to the chairperson if there is one. Even a glance is usually sufficient to drop the hint to the chairperson and have him or her intervene on your behalf;

- interrupt after a reasonable period and firmly ask: 'Is there a question?';

- when the rambler stops, try to pull out part of a question, re-phrase it and give a short answer;

- if there is no question, as soon as the rambler pauses, just say 'Thank you' and move on.

To assist you in answering questions, a checklist is provided. Read through it and use it along with the many other checklists provided in this handbook.

After the presentation—icing on the cake

CHECKLIST FOR HANDLING QUESTIONS

O **Listen carefully** to the question. Write down key elements so you don't miss points (most questions are multiple questions in effect).

O Always **let the questioner finish**. Don't cut in unless they are going on for a very long time, or making a speech with no question. Too many presenters are anxious to answer and jump in too early. They shouldn't interrupt you; don't interrupt questioners unless they are rambling.

O Make sure you understand the question. **Ask the questioner to clarify if you are not sure**.

O **Ask for the questioner's name** while you are collecting your thoughts. This allows you to address the person by name in a more personal way and makes him or her 'own' their question.

O Look at the questioner. **Establish eye contact**. After initial eye contact, you can glance around the audience, because you are, in effect, still talking to the whole audience.

O **Repeat the essence of the question** if you are in a large venue where people down the back or at the sides may not have heard the question.

O **Don't try to embarrass or make a fool of a questioner** no matter what they do or say.

O **Don't get into a two-way dialogue with one questioner**. Ask the questioner to discuss the matter with you later privately if it is turning into a discussion.

O **Don't use worn out cliches** such as 'I'm glad you asked me that' or 'That is a very good question'.

O **Encourage questions** from the audience. Lead them if you have to. Suggest areas or points for questions, eg, 'Is everyone clear on the policies in relation to...?'

O If you think it is necessary, **plant a colleague in the audience** to ask a pre-arranged question and stimulate questioning. Often it takes an ice-breaker to get the audience going.

O **Be concise**. Audiences will grow impatient with a presenter who uses question time to give another 15 minute talk. Questions are the audience's turn.

Evaluation

In today's age of accountability, quality assurance, benchmarking and international best practice, almost every aspect of management is evaluated in progressive companies, organisations and departments. There is no reason why presentations should be any different. Evaluation allows you to gain feedback which will help you fine-tune your presentation content and techniques.

There are a number of ways you can evaluate presentations. The most common method is asking audiences to fill out a survey form. Some conference and seminar organisers distribute speaker assessment forms as a matter of course. If this is done, ask for a copy of the feedback on your presentation. Usually the organisers will be happy to oblige.

Alternatively, you can prepare your own survey form. Most audiences will be willing to fill it out as people like to be asked for their opinions and advice. If you do design your own presenter's survey form, however, keep it short and simple. Returns will fall if it is too long or complex.

The following sample presenter's survey gives some suggested questions to evaluate both your presentation technique and achievement of your objectives.

Technology is also reshaping the way presenters evaluate their performances. Electronic audience monitoring systems provide a small keypad for either all or selected members of an audience and instant feedback and information can be gathered and collated on a central computer. A number of such systems are gradually coming into use.

Summary

○ Distribute handouts such as a copy of your script or notes to your audience after a presentation as this helps retention of your information.

○ Learn to identify the different types of questions. Understand the real motives behind questions and treat each type of question accordingly.

○ Never lose your cool in answering questions and never be rude or put anyone down—no matter how much you are provoked. Keep control of emotions that may be triggered by challenge, test and concealed objection questions.

○ Use the checklist for handling questions provided.

After the presentation—icing on the cake

PRESENTER'S SURVEY

On a scale of 1 to 5 (where 1 = very poor; 2 = poor; 3 = fair; 4 = good and 5 = excellent), circle a number to rate the speaker on the following:

Self-confidence	1	2	3	4	5
Clarity of voice. Could hear what he/she said	1	2	3	4	5
Conviction and enthusiasm	1	2	3	4	5
Well-structured presentation (Was it easy to follow?)	1	2	3	4	5
Eye contact with the audience	1	2	3	4	5
Avoided jargon and technical words	1	2	3	4	5
Visual materials	1	2	3	4	5
Held audience attention	1	2	3	4	5
Used natural, unaffected body language	1	2	3	4	5
Controlled nervous habits. List any:	1	2	3	4	5

....

....

Answered questions honestly and fully	1	2	3	4	5
Overall rating	1	2	3	4	5

What were the three main messages of the presentation?

1. ....

....

2. ....

....

3. ....

....

references

Bloomsbury. (1989) *Quotations for Speeches*. London: Bloomsbury Publishing.

Brody, Marjorie & Kent, Shawn. (1993) *Power Presentations*. New York, John Wiley & Sons.

Carnegie, Dale. (1957) *How to Develop Self-Confidence and Influence People Through Public Speaking*. London: Cedar Books.

Flacks, Niki, & Rasberry, Robert W. (1982) *Power Talk*. New York, The Free Press, Macmillan.

Hallan, Laila. (1993) 'Going over the top with overheads' in *Marketing*. May.

Macnamara, Jim & Venton, Breanda. (1990) *How To Give Winning Presentations*. Archipelago Press.

Malouf, Doug. (1983) *Confidence Through Public Speaking*. Melbourne, Information Australia.

Malouf, Doug. (reprinted 1988) *How to Create and Deliver a Dynamic Presentation*. Sydney: Simon & Schuster

Matthews, Janine. (1994) 'Good presenters are a breed apart' in *The Journal of the Australian Institute of Professional Communicators*. July.

McCormack, Mark. (1989) *Success Secrets*. London: Collins.

McMahon, Ed. (1986) *The Art of Public Speaking*. New York: Ballantine Books.

Morphew, Wayne. (1994) 'Communication: the key to getting ahead' in *Marketing*. May.

Oxford Dictionary of Quotations, 4th edition (1992). Oxford University Press.

Pease, Allan. (1981) *Body Language*. Sydney: Camel Publishing Company.

Stuart, Christina. (1988) *Effective Speaking*. New York: Pan Books.

Walters, Dottie & Walters Lilly. (1989) *Speak and Grow Rich*. London: Prentice Hall.

Wohlmuth, Ed. (1983) *The Overnight Guide to Public Speaking*. Philadelphia: Running Press.

*f*urther reading

Brandreth, Giles. (1983) *The Complete Public Speaker.* London, Sheldon Press.

Brown, Kenneth B. (1983) *Stand and Deliver.* Northamptonshire, Thorsons Publishers.

Dutton, John L. (1987) *How to be an Outstanding Speaker.* 2nd ed. Appleton, Wisconsin, Life Skills Publishing Company.

Gondin, W.R. & Mammen, E.W. (1975) *The Art of Speaking Made Simple.* London, W.H. Allen.

Hughes, Shirley. (1990) *Professional Presentations—A Practical Guide to the Preparation and Performance of Successful Business Presentations.* Sydney, McGraw-Hill.

Jay, Anthony. (1982) *Making Your Case.* Presentation series. UK, Video Arts Limited.

Leech, T. (1982) *How to Prepare, Stage and Deliver Winning Presentations.* New York, AMACOM (American Management Association).

Linkletter, Art. (1980) *Public Speaking for Private People.* New York, Bobbs-Merrill Co.

Linver, Sandy. (1978) *Speak Easy.* New York, Simon & Schuster.

Mears, A.G. (1979) *The Right Way to Speak in Public.* Surrey, Paperfronts.

Slaughter, T.M. (1988) *Project Yourself Like a Professional.* Kodak (Australasia) Pty Ltd.

Slaughter, T.M. (1990) *Teaching with Media.* University of Melbourne, Centre for Higher Education.

i n d e x

The modern presenter's handbook